God Still Loves My Kitchen

D1550611

DISTRIBUTED BY
CHOICE BOOKS
SALUNGA, PA. 17538
WE WELCOME YOUR RESPONSE

God Still Loves My Kitchen

MAB GRAFF HOOVER

ZONDERVAN
PUBLISHING HOUSE
OF THE ZONDERVAN CORPORATION | GRAND RAPIDS, MICHIGAN 49506

All Scripture, unless noted, is from the *New International Version* of the Holy Bible.

GOD STILL LOVES MY KITCHEN
© 1981 by The Zondervan Corporation
Grand Rapids, Michigan

Third printing 1982

Library of Congress Cataloging in Publication Data

Hoover, Mab Graff.
   God still loves my kitchen.

   1. Women—Prayer-books and devotions—English. I. Title.
BV4844.H66   242'.643   81-16488
ISBN 0-310-35622-9   AACR2

Designed by Martha Bentley
Edited by Louise H. Rock

Printed in the United States of America

Sincere thanks to Zondervan Publishing House
and their employees
for the help and encouragement they have given me,
especially to Louise Rock,
who gently sanded and polished my rough manuscript.

Special and loving thanks to my friends,
to each member of my family, and particularly to my husband.
Without them I would have had nothing to write.

All thanks and praise to the Lord Jesus Christ.
Without *Him* I could not write.

A Note to the Reader

Hi! I'm Mab Graff Hoover and I'd like to say hello, and thank you!, to you my readers. I've been very happy and thankful about the response to my first book, *God Loves My Kitchen Best,* and I hope that you will enjoy my new book as well.

If you laughed at my blunders in the first book, you'll like *God Still Loves My Kitchen* too—because, unfortunately, 'though I'm getting older, it's not always apparent that I'm getting wiser!

In one area, however, I believe the Lord has given me wisdom. And that is in regard to heaven. Several years ago I read in the Bible that I was a sinner, and that Jesus Christ died on the cross so that my sins could be forgiven. I believed what I read, and accepted Him. Now, because of his sacrifice (and not my goodness), I know I am going to heaven when I die.

Perhaps this book will give you a few smiles, but I hope that it also encourages you to respond to Jesus Christ, who can give you eternal life.

Contents

January

Thinking It Through with Flu

"I'b sorry, fa'bly," I said, as I flopped on the couch. "I can'd fix breakfast. Too sick—(cough, cough). Flu."

There were a few sympathetic remarks, then the family went to work in the kitchen, and I shivered under the afghan. My eyeballs ached as I looked at the worn-out Christmas tree. I had planned to take it down while I watched the Rose Bowl Parade, but I was too sick to even tell the kids the bacon was burning.

This was not the way I had planned to spend New Year's Day. The night before I had made a lot of resolutions: I was going to start jogging this very day; I was going to get all my Thank-You notes written; I was going to balance the checkbook and pay bills; I was going to run over to the mall and exchange my gifts; I was going to start *the diet*. . .

The thought of all these rules and regulations made me feel nauseated. I have never been good at keeping resolutions. No matter how strong my convictions on New Year's Eve, some ogre inside me talks me out of them by the end of the first week. Weak-willed—that's me.

In the middle of a chest-splitting cough, I thought of a way to make my weakness work for me. Maybe, if my New Year's resolutions were *keepable,* I would keep them! Although my head ached with the effort, I stretched to reach a Christmas card on the coffee table. On the back I scrawled my new New Year's vows:

1

1. *I will not jog,* or do any physical exercise unless it appeals to me and doesn't hurt.
2. *I will not* write Thank-You letters unless I want to.
3. *I will allow* my husband to pay the bills and balance the checkbook, even if he doesn't want to.
4. *I will not* wash windows. No, not one.
5. *I will not allow* myself to say yes to anyone who asks me to serve on a committee.
6. *I will refuse* to stay awake for one hour after lunch.
7. *I will not* waste my time by consulting the calorie chart.
8. *I will be content* with whatever there is to eat, even if it's fattening.

I tried to think of two more so I would have ten—but goodness knows these will be hard enough to keep. I'm almost glad I got the flu. If I had been jogging, or out exchanging gifts, I would never have come up with such a good set of resolutions!

I do not understand what I do. For what I want to do I do not do, but what I hate I do. (Rom. 7:15)

Rules, regulations and resolutions are impossible to keep! But Jesus puts *His* strength in *my* backbone.

I can do everything through him who gives me strength. (Phil. 4:13)

Delinquent Decoration

You know what really aggravates me? Here it is January. The holidays are over, thank goodness, and Christmas is the farthest thing from my mind. I was settled down on the couch with a cup of coffee to make an important decision. Should I get dressed and go to a white sale, or make my husband help me change the furniture around?

I looked up at the ceiling for better concentration, and there it was. A Christmas decoration I had forgotten to take down. I looked at that bell with a piece of dried-up mistletoe in it, and fumed. Every year I try so hard to get *all* the Christmas junk put away at one time. This battle has been going on ever since I got married. I remember after our first Christmas, I took down our little tree, carefully wrapped the ornaments, and saved each piece of tinsel. I swept the rug with a broom, because we didn't own a vacuum sweeper, and after I dusted I was so proud of our little house. What a relief to get all the Christmas clutter put away! A week later a neighbor asked if I was going to leave the wreaths in the windows all year.

Other Januarys, long after the tree is down, I have found red plastic poinsettias in the plants, green candles on the mantle, reindeer cutouts in the hall, and sleigh bells outside the front door. One year, when our mailbox was out by the street, the post looked like a barber pole until February.

This year I was determined to put away all the ornaments and decorations on the same day. I scrutinized every room. I took all the plant decorations out of the pots and washed them. I took down every Christmas card. I remembered to bring in the bells. I put away the old plastic nativity set in the hall as well as the new ceramic one. I vacuumed so thoroughly that even with my glasses on I couldn't find one pine needle or a speck of glitter. Ah-hah! At last I had done it. And then I found that moldy mistletoe.

While I was standing there with my eyes squeezed shut, my face getting red as I tried not to have a fit—guess what? A kiss was bestowed on my compressed lips by none other than my one and ornery.

I just may forget that decoration until next Christmas!

Are not two sparrows sold for a penny? Yet not one of them will fall to the ground apart from the will of your Father. And even the very hairs of your head are all numbered. (Matt. 10:29–30)

Sometimes, when I think of this world full of people, and that there is no end to the universe, I'm tempted to think God couldn't possibly know or care about me—but the Bible says He knows *all* my ways! (See Psalm 139.) He will not forget me when He calls the saints home!

Jesus, remember me when you come into your kingdom. (Luke 23:42)

Your Analysis, Doctor

"How long has it been since you've been to a doctor?" my mother asked.

"Hmm. Not since we moved," I answered. "Couple of years."

"You'd better have a check-up."

I knew she was right, and I promised to make an appointment.

The next week in the waiting room I was so nervous I read the opening of a story three times. Finally the nurse called me, and in the examining room she took my blood pressure and temperature, then handed me a paper gown.

"Take off everything but your shoes," she sang as she left me alone.

I hid my lingerie under my slacks and blouse, and put on the blue gown. It was much colder in the room than I first thought. I began to shake uncontrollably, and the frightening surroundings didn't help. A grotesque black and white table with chrome stirrups almost filled the tiny room, and its many drawers were sure to hold instruments of torture. My mouth felt as dry as toast and my deodorant failed as I sat on the icy stool, waiting.

After thirty minutes doctor and nurse breezed in. He was studying a chart and mumbling to himself: "Blood pressure okay; temp okay, urinalysis okay—"

"Pardon?" I interrupted. He frowned at me, then at the nurse.

"Whose chart is this?" he accused.

She looked startled. They both hurried out the door. I snatched off the gown and leaped into my clothes. Silently, I ran down the hall, through the reception room, and out into the bright sunshine.

I know Mother will ask me if I've been to the doctor. Should I say yes or no?

For we are the temple of the living God. (2 Cor. 6:16)

What an experience! I hate to make another appointment—and yet, anybody can make a mistake. It will be a big mistake if I neglect this wonderful body where the *Lord* lives.

I am fearfully and wonderfully made. (Ps. 139:14)

Company Manners

I used to think my husband never noticed how much I had to do, or how I got my work done. It wasn't until we invited his sister and brother-in-law for dinner a couple of months ago that I realized how observant he is.

As soon as he asked the blessing he said, "Sure glad you came. She's been knocking herself out on this meal all day." He squeezed my arm and grinned. "We haven't eaten like this since last Christmas!"

Then later on, we had a couple come down from San Luis Obispo, and he told them, "It's a good thing you didn't change your mind about coming. She's been working her head off for you. She even cleaned the oven! And bought a new bath set!"

Last week we got word that this couple from Denver was coming, so I rented a carpet shampooer. I had the ridiculous notion my husband would volunteer, but he asked, "Why do you work so hard when we have company?"

"Why?" I pointed to the dark place in front of his chair and the path that led across the carpet into the kitchen. "Because I wouldn't want them to see this dirty house! And *please,* honey, please don't tell them how hard I had to work, okay?"

"Why not?"

"Because I'd rather they would think I keep the house clean all the time than give me credit for a big job of housecleaning. It embarrasses me to think I let things go so long. So don't blab!"

I was still dressing when Tom and Louise arrived, and I could hear them talking as my husband showed them around our house.

"What a darling place," Louise said. "Spick and span! I just know she went to too much trouble for us!" (I beamed with delight.)

"Not a bit!" my husband said. "This little place practically keeps itself. She barely turned a hand." (The clod!)

During dinner (which I had slaved over—rump roast, mashed potatoes and gravy, corn, green beans, combination salad, hot rolls, and carrot cake), Tom said, "Terrific dinner, Mab. You must have worked all day."

"Oh no," my husband put up his hand and shook his head. "Women have it easy today. Most of this stuff is ready-to-serve. Right, love?"

I can't decide if he's stupid, or just plain ornery.

Do not think of yourself more highly than you ought, but rather think of yourself with sober judgment, in accordance with the measure of faith God has given you. (Rom. 12:3)

It's easy for me to wave away compliments and credits —unless I *don't* get them. Then I discover again how self-centered I am.

Let him who boasts boast in the Lord. (1 Cor. 1:31)

Two Teeny Tots

Every now and then it's good for us mothers of older children to take care of toddlers. It not only makes us thankful for our own kids just as they are, but also stiffens our resolve to never, never have any more!

We took care of my best girl friend's two teeny tots (and their dog) over the weekend. Since that family moved out of town, I call the two youngest children the Cucamonga Cuties. This morning my back feels as though I've been the victim of a hit-run accident.

I forgot how much you have to lift little ones and how helpless they are—well, not really helpless. All they had to do was let out a scream and the whole family came running. Both of them were delighted when they discovered this. They screamed piercingly about every fifteen minutes during their stay.

To keep their shrill screams from scaring the neighbors, I took them to a local amusement park, but the teenies were not amused. Teeny Boy hid his face in my lap all during the Affection Training School and loudly refused to touch Samantha, the friendly python. When he did take his face out of my lap, he thought the kids behind him were much more interesting than the exotic animals in front of him. Before I realized it, Teeny Girl opened a gate marked "Attendants Only" and three goats escaped. Immediately I decided that would be a good time for us to make our escape, so with a firm grip on the rascals, we hurried away.

Suddenly, Teeny Boy jerked loose and shouted, "I hold my *own* hand!" I just about had a heart attack as I saw him disappear in the crowd. But in an instant he was back beside me, strutting along with chubby arms folded.

At home I was looking forward to them taking a long nap so I could catch my breath and start dinner. They had just gone to sleep when their dog, which was outside, began to bark, loud and fast. I rushed out to the backyard, rolling a newspaper as I ran. But before I could bop him on the snout, he leaped in the air, snatched it out of my hand, and raced across the yard, shaking his head fiercely. When he had torn the paper to shreds, he looked at me invitingly and barked his joy that I was there to play. Of course the teenies woke up, howling and unconsolable.

That night Teeny Boy wanted to sleep with my husband, but he didn't want me in the bed. I couldn't have slept much anyway, because Teeny Girl had to have the light on all night.

When their parents came home, my friend said, "How can I ever thank you for taking care of them?"

I haven't told her yet, but it would be thanks enough if she takes care of our cat for three weeks in August.

Even a child is known by his actions, by whether his conduct is pure and right. (Prov. 20:11)

It's not easy to raise children. As I look back (and feel my aching back), I realize it was the Lord's strength that kept me on the job when ours were teeny tots.

Her children arise and call her blessed. (Prov. 31:28)

On Top of Everything

Why don't manufacturers design things with sloped tops? That way it would be impossible for me to pile things on every surface. I have chronic litterosis—"never put away today what might be used tomorrow" is my motto.

This morning, as I looked around my kitchen, I could not see one flat surface that wasn't piled up with stuff. Do other women keep bath towels (not folded), hair clippers, dog food, a basketball, muddy bedroom slippers, and the Sears catalog on their washer-dryer? Every bit of counter space is covered too, with anything from a dead African violet (it might revive) to a free sample of Tang. On the table there are library books, the telephone bill, coffee mugs, my purse, and two days' junk mail.

This clutter really bothers me, but somehow I can't seem to make myself keep things neat. If company is coming, or if none of us can find anything, then I fly into the housework like a whirlwind. Windows and curtains get washed, floors are scrubbed and waxed, bathroom fixtures get polished. Sometimes I even vacuum the furniture. During these fits of cleanliness, the cats, who usually sleep wherever they please, are terrified, and scoot from room to room with their ears out sideways. In their panic to get away from the vacuum, they race to the kitchen and skid past the refrigerator before they can get traction on the freshly waxed floor.

As soon as the reason for cleaning is over, even though I enjoy everything neat and beautiful, I lapse into my slovenly, littering ways. My good self and my rotten self argue continually.

"Why can't you hang up your clothes *now?*" Goodie whispers.

"Because I flat-out do not want to," Rotten snorts.

"But you like things neat. Now go clean out the oven before the grease burns. It will be easier."

"Let 'er burn," growls Rotten.

"You should at least vacuum today."

"Why? With shag carpeting who knows what's down there?"

Underneath all that junk mail I found a letter from friends back east. They're coming for a visit in about two weeks. Guess I'd better clean off the washer-dryer first.

They refused to give up their evil practices and stubborn ways. (Judg. 2:19)

Me? Stubborn? Yes. The Bible has already shown me that God's plan is for me to be orderly, because He is a God of order. When will I learn that housekeeping is a matter of putting God *first?*

Do not be like the horse or the mule, which have no understanding. (Ps. 32:9)

12

Hold the Phone

When my husband saw our latest phone bill, we had a few words. In fact, he threatened to have it disconnected if I don't cut out some of the toll calls.

"Is it my fault half our friends and relatives have moved out of our area?" I yipped. "How can I keep in touch?"

"I don't mind you keeping in touch," he growled. "It's your in-depth coverage that's getting to me." He slapped the phone bill. "Cucamonga, $2.45!"

"She's my dearest friend!" I glared at him. "Anyway, it's not just social calls that run up the bill. Every time I make a business call, they put me on hold."

He didn't believe me, but it's the truth.

Yesterday, for instance, I was trying to find a fingerprint set for a nephew who is into detective stuff. I looked in the Yellow Pages, but all I could find was *fingernails,* so I called this big department store which is just far enough away to be a toll call.

When the switchboard operator answered, before I could even say hello, she put me on hold. When she came back on she said, "That line is still busy; will you hold?"

"What line?" I asked.

"The line you wanted!" she snapped.

"I haven't even talked to you yet."

"If you'll simply tell me what you want, I can ring."

"Okay, I'm looking for a—"

13

"Excuse me, will you hold?"

I looked at the silent receiver and tried to decide if I should hang up or hang on. When she came back (about five message units later) she said, "Did they answer?"

"Who?"

"Oh, no—it's you. What did you want?"

When I told her she said, "That would be Toys. I'll ring."

When Toys finally (seven rings) answered, the toy lady said, "No—I think that would be Crafts. They handle finger painting."

"Uh—what I'm looking for is more like detectives use."

"I'll transfer you to Security. Will you hold?"

I remember thinking before I hung up that I'm sure glad it isn't this hard to get through to the Lord.

Well, if my husband does have the telephone disconnected, maybe I'll lose some weight. I'll have to get out to make some of these contacts, instead of letting my fingers do the walking through the Yellow Pages.

Then you will call upon me and come and pray to me, and I will listen to you. (Jer. 29:12)

I am definitely going to cut back on telephoning friends and relatives—but I am glad I don't have to cut back on my calls to the Lord.

When I call, answer me quickly. (Ps. 102:2)

February

My Heart Belongs to Chocolate

I hope my husband doesn't give me a box of candy this Valentine's. Every year I just get on a good diet after the Christmas cramming, and then February 14 arrives and he gives me a heart-shaped box of chocolates.

Of course I wouldn't ask him *not* to bring candy—because it might hurt his feelings! I certainly wouldn't want him to quit thinking of me as his valentine. I have two girl friends whose husbands never remember their birthdays, much less Valentine's Day. I'm glad he loves me enough to buy a gift, but I can't help wishing he would bring me earrings, or perfume, a plant—even a pair of pantyhose —anything that would be an incentive to stay on my diet. But when I see that beautiful red heart, with its pink satin ribbon, and know there are *chocolates* inside, all my will power fades. Once I start in on those forbidden fondants it takes about two months and five pounds to get myself psyched up to go on a diet again. I'm so addicted to chocolate I even like chocolate-flavored yogurt!

Oh, candy makers of America! Why don't you have a heart, and make us some *good* tasting, low calorie sweets? How about chocolate coated carrot sticks? Or coconut covered cottage cheese balls dipped in chocolate? Or dried zucchini that looks and tastes like a Mr. Goodbar? But I know that wouldn't really solve the problem, because I would still crave chocolate. I wish I could be hypnotized and told that I hate chocolate. Wouldn't that be great?

"When I clap my hands," the hypnotist would say, "you will no longer love chocolate. From now on you will hate dark chocolate crammed with pecans; light chocolate filled with candied pineapple; chocolate creme centers dipped in chocolate. Syrupy, cherry chocolates will turn your stomach and chocolate coated almond clusters will have no appeal."

What a dream! An impossible dream. I know I will always love chocolate.

Well—you know the old saying, "God give me the serenity to accept the things I cannot change." So I guess if my sweet husband wants to give me chocolates, I might as well relax and enjoy them.

"Everything is permissible for me"—but not everything is beneficial. "Everything is permissible for me"—but I will not be mastered by anything. (1 Cor. 6:12)

How can I say I have crucified this flesh, and also say I am addicted to chocolate? What is wrong? *My thoughts.* Even before temptation is present I have said *yes* to chocolate and *no* to—*Christ!*

Those controlled by the sinful nature cannot please God. (Rom. 8:8)

Happy Un-Birthday, George

It was probably because of a patriotic school program we attended, or maybe it was the discussion we had about the government changing traditional dates, but whatever it was, I dreamed I had a talk with George Washington.

"Mr. President," I said, "or would you rather be called George?"

"George is all right," he said graciously.

"Sir, my calendar says that the eighteenth—"

His cheeks began to get red and the ruffle around his neck trembled.

"Are you all right, sir?"

"Carry on!" he growled.

"Mr. President—George, sir. It's a historical fact that you were born on February twenty-second. Does it bother you that we've changed your birth date?"

"Most certainly!" he snapped. "Would you like to have your birthday changed?"

"No sir. I really wouldn't. I don't know why they do it."

"Ah, well," he said, cooling down. "I suppose it's jolly good they even remember me. The year 1732 was a long time ago."

"We'll never forget you, sir, George. After all, you're the Father of Our Country."

"Jove! Are they still teaching that?"

"Of course!"

"I thought p'raps the bloody feminists would be insisting that Martha get equal credit, and that I be referred to as the 'Person' of our country."

"Hey! Actually, George, that's a good idea. We should also be celebrating Martha's birthday."

His blue eyes looked cold, so I decided to change the subject.

"Sir, if you had the opportunity, would you trade places with today's president?"

He shook his head so violently his white hair flipped in his eyes. "My word, *no*! I had problems with the French, the Indians, and Martha, but they were a cup of tea compared to your crime, inflation, and pollution."

"It's been an honor to talk to you, Mr. President. I, for one, will hang out my flag not only on the eighteenth, but also on the twenty-second. Now, one last question: Is it true you have never told a lie?"

His smile resembled the Mona Lisa. "Ask no more questions—and I'll tell you no lies."

What a man was George Washington!

Righteousness exalts a nation, but sin is a disgrace to any people. (Prov. 14:34)

If George Washington was alive today, his heart would break over America's corruption. But what can I, one person, do to keep our country great? Cling, hold fast, to the faith of our fathers.

As I was with Moses, so I will be with you. (Josh. 1:5)

A Dangerous Game

The first thing I noticed after we stepped through the huge, ornate door and sank into thick carpeting, was an overpowering smell—the smell of sweaty T-shirts. Loud rock music didn't cover the incessant *crack-whack-smack* of balls being smashed against plaster.

We were in the lobby of a new health club, guests of Cathy, who had lost her heart, mind, and pocketbook to the game of racquetball.

"You'll love it!" she said, a wild light in her eyes.

"I don't want to play," I whined. "Can't I watch for a while?"

She shrugged, and we sat down on a leather couch which faced a glass court where four fellows crouched, leaped, rolled, and ran around insanely.

The object was to smack a little blue ball with something that looked somewhat like a tennis racquet, except with a shorter handle. They moved so fast and so ferociously I was certain one of them would be killed at any moment. They were glistening with sweat—their T-shirts were soaked, their heads were dripping, their shorts—I almost gagged to think what it smelled like inside that vault.

"Doesn't it look fun?" Cathy yelled. "Come on upstairs!"

I followed her up carpeted stairs and across a wide cat-walk where we could look down on courts on either side. Several games were in progress, the players locked in windowless rooms. All of them, except a couple who looked to be very much in love, were attacking the ball and their opponent so savagely it scared me.

"Looks to me like a person could get hurt!" I yelled.

Cathy nodded.

"I got smashed in the face one night, so now I wear goggles," she screamed at me. "But you're safe up here."

"Thank goodness!" I called, just as a ball came rocketing straight up at me and smacked my arm.

"I don't think this game is for me," I mumbled, as I rubbed the red spot.

Outside, I took a deep breath of clean air.

"I'm sure you'd like it if you'd try it," Cathy said.

I nodded vaguely. But I thought to myself, *One person's racquet isn't necessarily another person's ball.*

[*Jesus said,*] *Come with me by yourselves to a quiet place and get some rest.* (Mark 6:31)

I need more exercise than I'm getting, and I should make a decision, but unless a sport can fit in our budget, and be fun and relaxing, then I'm not going out for it—even if it is the "in" thing to do.

One decision I'm glad I have already made: to let Jesus Christ be my Savior. To put off that decision is to play a dangerous game.

There remains, then, a . . . rest for the people of God. Let us, therefore, make every effort to enter that rest. (Heb. 4:9, 11)

TV or Not TV

"Honey!" I called to my husband. "There's a man at the door who wants to know if we'll sign up for pay TV."

"Tell him to come back later," he answered. "We'll talk about it first."

The fellow gave me a four-color brochure on the enchantments of first-run movies.

"These do sound exciting," I said later to my husband. "I'd like to see some of these movies."

"There must be seven hundred movies on regular TV you haven't seen yet," my husband commented. "You always fall asleep."

"Well! I can't help it if TV hypnotizes me."

"So why should we pay, when you sleep so well for free?"

"But just think—there wouldn't be any commercials."

"That's no advantage," he said. "At least you wake up during commercials and get us something to eat. We don't need pay TV. Anyhow, the guys at work say the movies are raw sex."

"But we wouldn't have to watch the trash. *I'm* not addicted to TV. *You* always have it on."

"Me?" He gave me his astonished-innocent look. "You're the one who turns it on every evening."

"Yes, but you're the one who is glued to it," I pouted. "You never talk to me anymore."

He leaped up and snapped off *Little House on the Prairie.*

"Okay," he growled. "Let's talk."

I never realized before how long two minutes of silence could be.

"We could read," I said carefully.

"Reading puts *me* to sleep."

"How about a game of Scrabble?"

"How about Cribbage?" he countered.

"You know I can't add fast enough."

"Monopoly?"

"Takes too long. Checkers?"

More silence. We looked at the third party, watching us from across the room. My husband stood up, stretched, casually walked over, and flipped its switch.

"When did you say that pay TV fellow would be back?"

"He didn't say," I answered. I yawned and snuggled down in the afghan for the nine o'clock movie.

You must no longer live as the Gentiles do, in the futility of their thinking. They are darkened in their understanding. . . . (Eph. 4:17–16)

I am ashamed of myself to think I would even consider signing up for pay TV. It would be giving Satan an invitation to show us his vile merchandise every night.

And do not give the devil a foothold. (Eph. 4:27)

Wild Imagination

Sometimes I wish I didn't have such a wild imagination. It's all right when I am telling the kids stories, or trying to get out of a jam, but when I am looking for something which is lost, I wish my imagination would be quiet, and let my brain present just the facts.

Example: I have looked for my blue Papermate pen for two weeks. My imagination has sent me on all sorts of fruitless foraging, and every time, before I looked, I received a clear mental picture which showed me exactly where that ball point was hiding.

"I'll tell you where it is," Imagination promised one day. *Remember? The last time you used it was when you paid bills!"*

"Of course!" I visualized it in the middle section of my purse, next to the checkbook. I dumped everything out of my pocketbook. It was a sickening mess—but no pen.

"Ah!" Imagination yelped, snapping my fingers. *"Now I remember! You used it for your Bible lesson."* I raced to the coffee table, threw the newspaper to the floor, and grabbed my Bible. A yellow pencil rolled slowly to the edge and fell off.

Seated on the floor, with legs crossed, I tried to concentrate. I could see the pen in my mind—royal blue, with chrome point and two little hearts on the clip.

"It's lying on the third shelf of the linen closet," Imagination whispered.

"But why is it in the linen closet?"

"Not for you to reason why," Imagination stated. *"Go."*

With eyes closed and hands outstretched I proceeded to the linen closet. With confidence I yanked open the door and a stack of towels fell on my head. The pen was not on the third shelf. Or any shelf.

Maybe my imagination isn't wild enough. I found the pen this morning. Never, in my wildest . . . , would I have thought to look in the desk drawer where it belongs.

For the L ORD searcheth all hearts, and understandeth all the imaginations of the thoughts. (1 Chron. 28:9 KJV)

There was a lawyer who sat in his office and stared at the bank across the street. Every day he imagined how he could rob it. He imagined every detail. At last he had to try it. Now he is in prison.

Finally, brothers, whatever is true, whatever is noble, whatever is right, whatever is pure, whatever is lovely, whatever is admirable—if anything is excellent or praiseworthy—think about such things. (Phil. 4:8)

Me Meek?

I resented it the other day when a friend told me I was weak-willed. We were having lunch together and I told her about an experience I had at the check-out counter at the Super Market.

"I had a basket full of stuff, and was almost to the cashier when I turned around and saw this fellow behind me with a quart of milk. 'Go ahead of me,' I said, and he smiled and thanked me. Then I glanced over my shoulder and there was this tired-looking mother with a squirming baby in one arm and a loaf of bread in the other. Of course, I told her to go ahead."

My friend snorted.

"That's two. How many more?"

"Well," I continued, "behind her was this young fellow, all greasy and hot looking, holding a bag of Twinkies and a can of pop. I let him by—and I have to admit, I was getting a little irritated by then—and a little old man limped up with just a single head of cabbage—"

"You didn't let him go ahead of you, did you?"

"But he was so old, and seemed to be in a hurry."

"But letting all those people go by made you late meeting *me* for lunch!"

"I know—I don't know why I'm so tender-hearted and polite."

"Seems to me more like you're namby-pamby and meek!"

27

Namby-pamby? Meek? Me? Hah! I thought angrily. *From now on I'll be strong-willed and assertive.*

"Let's forget it," she said. "What are you going to order for lunch?"

"Just a small salad," I answered. "I'm dieting."

"Dieting? Why do you want to diet? You need more than salad. Order the enchilada plate with me."

The enchiladas were delicious, but I'm still mad at my friend. I may be a little bit meek, but namby-pamby? Never!

Being strengthened with all power according to his glorious might so that you may have great endurance and patience. (Col. 1:11)

The Lord wants me to be kind, humble, and tender-hearted. But He doesn't want me to be a doormat.

You are all sons of God through faith in Christ Jesus. (Gal. 3:26)

A Hair-raising Fad

When blow dryers first became a fad I thought I had to have one. A good friend quit back-combing her hair and used a blow dryer. She looked so chic with her hair close to her head and swept back at the sides!

"Bouffant hair styles are *out,*" she advised. "You'll look much younger if you quit ratting your hair and use a dryer to style it."

I don't remember what I paid for my dryer, but whatever it was, it was too much. The thing lies in a drawer most of the time.

I tried to learn. I followed the instructions that came with it, but when I was through, my hair looked like a poodle before grooming.

"You need a good cut," my friend said. So I went to her stylist. When he was through snipping and shaping I didn't recognize myself. I had worn my hair high for years. Now my shorn, flat head looked like something out of *Star Wars.*

But my girl friend insisted that I looked much younger.

"Do I look young to you?" I asked my husband.

He looked at my head and narrowed his eyes.

"Hmmm—yeah—" He nodded. "A young boy."

"I'm sure I'll look better when I learn how to use the blow dryer," I said. "Can I practice on you?"

Reluctantly, he washed his hair and sat down at the kitchen table.

I tried to look professional as I twirled the thing nonchalantly, but before I knew what was happening I blasted him
in the eye with hot air, and blew sugar all over the table.

"How much longer?" he complained. "I'm getting a
headache."

When I was finished, his hair was puffed out evenly all
over his head. He looked at himself and groaned, "I look
like a half-eaten mushroom!"

He wouldn't let me practice any more, so I had to work on
myself. Every time I would get one place to look just right, I
would blow it all to pieces trying to work on another section.
I felt like a cat trying to groom herself in front of a fan.

I never have learned to style my hair with the thing. Once
in a while I use the dryer, but mostly it stays in the drawer,
with the hair frosting bonnet and the false fingernail kit.

*If anyone says to you, "Look, here is the Christ!" or, "There
he is!" do not believe it. For false Christs and false prophets
will appear. (Matt. 24:23–24)*

There is nothing wrong with owning a blow dryer for
those who want to use them, but I must be on guard to not
spend money for things simply because they are a new
fad. They may not be better for *me* than the old way. The
Bible says I must also be on guard against new religions
which may claim to do more for me than my old-time
religion, which is faith in Jesus Christ.

---

*Contend for the faith that was once for all entrusted to the
saints. (Jude 3)*

 March

Bike Fright

Now that spring has come, my husband has talked me into a new venture. At least, it's new to me—bike riding. He is very good at it. He can even sit on the handlebars backwards and pump nonchalantly, while I wobble along behind him. I never had a bike when I was young, but it's probably just as well because I've never been good at athletics. If I had owned a bike I might have killed myself.

"Did you know your daughter lacks coordination?" the PE teacher asked my mother one day as she wiped blood off my shin, which I had kicked instead of the soccer ball.

"Well—we knew she was the most awkward one in the family—" Mother answered.

"She may not outgrow it," the teacher went on, "but ballet lessons might help."

Mother signed me up for six lessons to see if it was worth it, but that teacher suggested I drop out. I could never get in first position without falling over.

"Don't waste time trying to teach me to ride a bike," I said to my husband after I told him about my uncoordinated past.

"Forget all that," he said. "Look to the future. You can learn to ride as well as anybody!"

So far, under his guidance, we've only pedaled around our own block. He always takes the lead and I'm glad, because then he can't see some of the dumb things I do.

For example, I can turn to the left just fine, but for some reason when I turn right I lose control and wobble out into the middle of the street. (I wish I could apologize to the terrified driver of a cream-colored Lincoln who had to swerve to keep from hitting me.)

My bike is only a three-speed, but as far as I'm concerned it's a two-speed—too slow and too fast. I can't quite get the hang of putting on the brakes with my hands. If I need to brake, most of the time I just sit there hypnotized, full speed ahead, with damp, limp hands. But if we're riding along nicely with the breeze blowing out our shirt tails, I might squeeze the handles just because I'm happy. So far I've only dumped myself once.

I'm trying to take my husband's advice and forget about the uncoordinated things I've done in the past. My goal is to be able to bike to the supermarket by next month. And I'll do it, too—if everybody stays out of my way.

... But one thing I do: Forgetting what is behind and straining toward what is ahead, I press on toward the goal to win the prize for which God has called me heavenward in Christ Jesus. (Phil. 3:13–14)

Whether in the physical realm or the spiritual realm, nothing is as devastating to our progress as dwelling on past failures.

Let us throw off everything that hinders ... and let us run with perseverance the race marked out for us. (Heb. 12:1)

Hanging Loose

"I think I might paper the dining room this spring," I murmured to my husband as he watched the news. "Okay?"

We have this routine where I ask for his approval on something, and if he doesn't answer, I figure it's okay to go ahead. If it doesn't turn out right I can always claim that I asked him. And then he can claim he never heard me.

He didn't answer about the wallpaper, so tomorrow I think I'll go look at patterns. I love wallpaper, and I have done quite a bit of papering. I have made a few normal mistakes, such as getting it on crooked, or upside down, but I have also learned from my mistakes.

The first whole bedroom I papered I learned I should have listened to my step-dad, who hung paper for a living. "Be sure and size that room," he warned, "or you'll never get paper to stick on that high-gloss enamel."

I bought the sizing and mixed it up, but by the time I sloshed a little on the wall and a lot on me, I decided he probably was too cautious. I dumped it out and proceeded to paper the room with beautiful, tulip-covered paper. The next morning the whole room looked like a giant tulip—with wallpaper petals unfolding gracefully all around!

I was a little discouraged, but after I got the strips back up with masking tape I decided to do the middle bedroom. Sears was having a sale on pre-pasted paper, guaranteed to stick.

"Are you sure that's enough?" the clerk asked, when I put four double rolls on the counter.

"Sure," I said. "I've done this before."

"Well, I thought I'd ask. . . This paper is a close-out."

I must have measured wrong, and besides that, one whole piece got ruined when it stuck to itself. Of course there was no more at Sears. So I used a piece of gift wrap that was almost the same pattern, but there was still an area about three feet by four not papered.

But, one learns from these experiences, doesn't one?

Perhaps this one has learned it would be more fun to read tomorrow than shop for wallpaper.

Listen to advice and accept instruction, and in the end you will be wise. (Prov. 19:20)

I seldom ask for advice, and if I do, I usually don't follow it. I don't follow instructions very well either, but think *my* way is better. Could it be I have a touch of the *"I wills"*?

The fear of the LORD is the beginning of knowledge, but fools despise wisdom and discipline. (Prov. 1:7)

With Pin in Hand

"Why do you have a clothespin on this light bill?" my husband asked as he rummaged through the desk for a pencil.

"Don't you see it has the check clipped to it?" I answered. "I can't find the box of paper clips."

"Why don't you mail it?"

"Because I can't find a stamp right now."

Later on he said, "Here's a paper clip on the drape."

"Don't touch it!" I yelped. "That's holding the hem in until I can find a safety pin."

"I thought you had a bunch of safety pins the other night when you were curling your wig."

"Not a bunch. Just two, and I need those to hold the wig on the styrofoam head."

"What happened to those long ones that came with it?"

I gave him a hateful look.

How do I know what happened to those pins? How do I know what happens to anything? There must be secret compartments in this house with invisible monsters who steal all my things. No matter what I'm looking for—a certain magazine, a can of oregano, my pink half-slip—all, vanished. Just recently I was going to set my hair with bobby pins for a change. I *know* that somewhere in the bathroom I used to have an old Sucrets box full of bobby pins, but do you think I could find one single pin? I finally went outside and took the few I leave on the clothesline (somehow all the clothespins have disappeared)—but there weren't enough to even pin up one side, so I had to use paper clips.

Hey! That's it! The paper clips are in the bathroom.

Then they can train the younger women to love their husbands and children, to be self-controlled and pure, to be busy at home, to be kind, and to be subject to their husbands, so that no one will malign the word of God. (Titus 2:4–5)

What? Could my sloppy housekeeping actually cause God's Word to be slandered?

For God is not a God of disorder. (1 Cor. 14:33)

Mañana

One morning my husband and I were eating breakfast and talking about inflation.

"I can't believe how prices have jumped in the last three years," he said. He held out his coffee cup for a refill. "How much a pound is this stuff now?"

When I told him, he choked, then sputtered. "We ought to boycott 'em! You can bet your boots if everybody quit drinking coffee for a month, the prices would come down." There was fire in his eyes as he took a big swallow. "You women do the buying. You could really sock it to 'em. Just quit buying coffee!"

Usually, as soon as he goes to work, I put on a fresh pot, but this morning, as I thought about how we consumers are manipulated, I got irritated.

"I'll just quit drinking coffee," I said. "I'll show 'em."

As soon as I made the decision I began to shake.

"Come on, stupid," I said to me. "You can't be having withdrawal symptoms already." But the long day ahead, with lots of work and no coffee, was a dismal thought. I couldn't sit around and think about it. Action! I decided to go visit my neighbor, and the wicked thought crossed my mind that she might offer me . . . (Get thee behind me, Satan!).

She did, but due to some contrariness in me, I lifted my chin and said, "No, thank you. I'm never going to drink coffee again until they lower prices." I glared at her. "If all of us would band together and refuse to buy it, prices would have to come down!" She batted her eyes sadly and looked away.

When I went home I felt as strong as Carrie Nation. I had actually turned down a cup of coffee! But I was miserable.

Nobly, I made coffee and watched my husband drink three cups of the delicious-smelling stuff during dinner.

I didn't sleep very well, and when morning came I had a horrible headache, and my hands shook as I cooked breakfast.

"What's wrong with you?" my husband asked. "Flu again?"

"Coffee," I croaked. "No coffee since we talked about it yesterday."

His eyes widened. Then he took me in his arms.

"Poor, poor baby!" He gave me a sip of his coffee. "Forget the boycott! After all, what can one person do?"

Who is going to harm you if you are eager to do good? But even if you should suffer for what is right, you are blessed. (1 Peter 3:13)

It probably wouldn't bring prices down if I quit drinking coffee. But what bothers me is that I wasn't willing to give it a try—yet I *am* willing to be manipulated by *somebody*, out there. Lord! Please give me the courage of my convictions.

Anyone . . . who knows the good he ought to do and doesn't do it, sins. (James 4:17)

Leave Off the Leftovers

Sunday's paper had a lot of recipes for using up leftovers. Just reading them made me a little sick.

For example, there was one to use up combination salad. The thought of all that leftover, limp lettuce lying in the bottom of a bowl is gross enough; but you're supposed to add tomato juice, garlic, vinegar, salad oil, green peppers, and a cucumber; dump it all in a blender; whip it up—and *drink* it.

Here's one for leftover peas: 1 can celery soup, 1 can tomato soup, 2 cups leftover codfish. Add leftover peas, then heat and serve. How's that for an appetizer?

None of the recipes appealed to me, and it's too bad, because my refrigerator is full of leftovers. I try not to be wasteful, but it's been my experience that I waste a lot of good ingredients trying to disguise some leftover the family rejected in the first place. Then the leftovers, instead of being used up, keep growing.

Besides that, I've lost my family's trust. My son will never eat anything now without first sniffing it, then asking, "What's in this?"

I'm sorry I'm not more innovative when it comes to leftovers. I guess I'm just not that interested in cooking. Even my hamburgers are tough, and I'm the only person I know whose instant potatoes get lumps.

However, that first recipe with the blender gives me an

idea. How about if I take the leftover tuna, those two slices of dry meat loaf, that dab of buttered carrots, the dish of vanilla pudding, and the rest of the Christmas cheese ball, put them in the blender with three or four eggs and some chili powder, and make a soufflé? Or I could leave out the chili powder and add oregano. Or sage. Garlic powder?

How about the garbage disposal?

One who is slack in his work is brother to one who destroys. (Prov. 18:9)

Now that I think about it, it's not as important to learn how to use up leftovers as it is to learn how to *cook* well enough so my family will eat it all the first time.

Whatever you do, work at it with all your heart, as working for the Lord, not for men. (Col. 3:23)

Guilty or Not Guilty?

Do other people feel as guilty about things as I do? I'm not talking about the times when I actually am guilty.

I am referring to the times when I'm innocent—for instance, last Saturday my husband was washing the car and asked me to step outside.

"Do you have any idea how that dent got in the grill?" he demanded, looking into my eyes. Although I didn't have a clue, my stomach flopped and my heart began to pound. I tried to look innocent, but began to blush. He looked at me even more suspiciously.

"Honestly!" I cried. "I don't know how it got there. And that's the truth!" Even my words made me sound guilty, because I read somewhere that when people add, "honest," or "that's the truth," what they are saying is probably false. I wasn't lying, but I was miserable as he stared at me.

I felt even more guilty the last time I was at the dentist's. The receptionist suddenly looked straight at me and said, "What's going on? Who took my stapler?"

Everyone looked at me. I quickly opened my arms to prove I didn't have it, but my hands trembled and my cheeks got hot. She kept looking at me. Just as I was on the verge of dumping everything out of my purse, she found the stapler under some papers.

Guilt is like an ugly fly—always hovering around. Have you ever been in a situation where they announce some money has been stolen? I always feel guilty. Or if someone shows me an object and says, "I wonder how this got broken?" I always feel it's my fault, even if I've never seen the thing before.

Why do I feel guilty? Sometimes I *am* guilty and need to get right with the Lord—but the other times, when I'm innocent, it must be Satan, that false accuser, poking holes in my joy bucket.

Who is my accuser? Let him confront me! It is the Sovereign Lord who helps me. (Isa. 50:8–9)

Guilt feelings are like running a temperature—an indication we need to be examined by the Physician.

All have sinned. (Rom. 3:23)

Easy for You—
Difficult for Me

Occasionally, when the sun has passed its equinox, the moon is fully illuminated, and the Milky Way has lost its chocolate, there comes a time when both kids are away for lunch. Yesterday was such a day, so I telephoned Gladys, a friend I used to work with, and made a date to meet her. It was great to see her. Except when she came out of her office, I felt frumpy and fat in my K-Mart special, and she looked slender and smashing in a new outfit.

"You've lost weight!" I cried.

"No I haven't," she said. "It must be this dress—I just made it."

"You *made* that?" And she works eight hours a day!

"It's exactly like one that cost $75.00 at the Broadway," she said with a chuckle. "I got the remnant for $7.00."

"Wish I could sew like that—but I can't."

"Of course you can. All you have to do is be careful to pick a pattern and material that will flatter your figure. Then follow the instructions."

"I've tried," I moaned. "I've never made anything I really like."

"Negative thinking!" She waggled her finger. "You *can* do it."

When she went back to work I wandered into a yard goods store. Maybe, if I was careful, I could make an elegant dress like hers.

45

I took at least ten minutes looking at patterns, then turned toward the gorgeous bolts of material. One thing I had learned about sewing was that vertical stripes make one look slimmer. I chose one with red, yellow, blue, and green stripes. I took the bolt and pattern to the clerk.

"Four yards, please."

She measured quickly, then cut and folded the material.

"Four yards at $6.98," she began as she wrote on a srcap of paper.

I gasped! I hadn't thought about the price.

"Pattern—thread, binding—mmm—comes to $31.93."

I stared at the figures. I had thought more like $7.00. In a moment of clairvoyance I visualized the expensive mess that material would be in my hands. I would not look smashing. I would look like a botched-up awning. All my past sewing failures marched before me: zippers whose ends did not match; scalloped hems, puckered seams, gaping necklines, upside down sleeves. I felt faint.

"I—I—can't—" I whimpered.

The clerk looked alarmed. "You can't pay?"

"I can't sew! I don't know what made me come in." I looked around wildly at the towering bolts of cloth. "I don't want it!" My voice rose. "I don't want it!"

"There, there," she said as to a child. "You don't have to buy it." She guided me toward the door. "We'll just put it over in that nice table of remnants." She gave me a firm little shove out the door.

In the car I made myself a promise. No more lunches with Gladys unless *she* promises to wear an old skirt and sweater.

If the whole body were an eye, where would the sense of hearing be? If the whole body were an ear, where would the sense of smell be? But in fact God has arranged the parts in the body, every one of them, just as he wanted them to be. (1 Cor. 12:17–18)

Doesn't the Bible say I can do *all* things through Christ? Yes. And I *can* sew—but not as well as Gladys. I can also sing in the choir, but I don't fret because I am not a soloist. In every area I must realize my limitations and concentrate on my best gift.

Now you are the body of Christ, and each one of you is part of it. (1 Cor. 12:27)

April

Old Story Resurrected

If any eggs are dyed this year, the kids will have to do them. I've boiled, dyed, and decorated more eggs than I want to think about, and after last year's egg hunt in our backyard, I said, *"No more!"* It wasn't so bad, I guess, except that our retriever kept bringing every egg to me as soon as I hid it, and I had to wash most of them. And then, the Cucamonga Cuties, Jeni and David, kept finding the same eggs at the same time. When the hunt was over, they were both crying. All the kids ate so many hardboiled eggs, jelly beans, and chocolates they didn't want any of the dinner I had slaved over.

All the goodies we traditionally prepare are supposed to be in joyful celebration of Christ's resurrection, but I don't think we talk about this great miracle of God enough. At least at our house, it seems everything centers around good food, eggs, and the Easter bunny.

This year, in the mall, there was a line of mothers and children waiting to speak to a gigantic pink rabbit, sitting on a white throne. I know the kids ask Santa for presents, but what could they have to say to the Easter Bunny? When I got closer I realized the kiddies were having their pictures taken on Bre'r Rabbit's lap.

Most of the tots didn't want to get close to him and pulled back in terror. One mother was trying to coax her frightened toddler to get in line.

"Don't you want to talk to the Easter Bunny?"

51

"No!" the child shrieked and struggled to get away.

"But don't you want him to bring you a pretty basket with lots of eggs in it?"

The child considered a moment, then began to howl.

"Mustn't hurt Bunny's feelings," Mommy insisted. "He knows what you think, and if you've been bad or good."

"Does she know the real Easter story?" I blurted out.

The mother looked as shocked as I felt.

What possessed me to say that? I think to myself when I recall this incident. But I went on.

"I mean, does she know that Jesus died on the cross and came back to life to prove we needn't be afraid of anything?"

"Goodness, no," the mother said imperiously. "That's too hard for her to understand."

Hmm. It seems to me it would be much easier for a child to believe God can do anything, than to believe a rabbit lays colored eggs and reads minds.

Since the children have flesh and blood, he too shared in their humanity so that by his death he might destroy him who holds the power of death—that is, the devil—and free those who all their lives were held in slavery by their fear of death. (Heb. 2:14–15)

I may relent and dye a few eggs, and I'll probably make a good dinner. But instead of an egg hunt, I think this year I'll have the kids read the Easter story according to Matthew, chapters 27 and 28.

After three days I will rise again. (Matt. 27:63)

Watch the Birdie

My latest hobby (besides eating out) is taking pictures. My family complains a lot because I'm always asking someone to pose. I don't have an expensive camera, either. But those things don't discourage me. I always have my little Minolta loaded and ready to shoot. As the mother of this family I feel it's my responsibility to keep a pictorial record. Besides, my dream is that someday I'll be at a dramatic happening—maybe a bank robbery or a fiery wreck, and I'll be the only one on the scene with a camera. I might take a picture worth hundreds of dollars! In fact, I thought I had that picture the other day.

I was going south on the Santa Ana Freeway and cars began to slow. I was sure something big had happened. I picked up the camera, checked the focus doohicky, and made sure the film was advanced. As we crept along, I was alert, ready to shoot the action. I saw a wrecker speed by on the shoulder; then I saw the Highway Patrol cars with their lights flashing. I put the camera to my eye—but when we got there all I could see was a couple of cars pulled over, policemen, and some other people standing around.

Traffic speeded up then, and I put the camera back on the seat. Suddenly, right beside me, was the most crunched-up car I'd ever seen! I grabbed at the camera, knocked it to the floor, and almost ran into the car ahead of me. I did take a picture, but when I got the roll developed I was disappointed to see I had only taken part of the window frame and a stretch of freeway fence. I'm sure there is something wrong with my camera, because I have several strange pictures like that.

My best pictures so far are of our animals sleeping, but my favorite is a darling one of the parakeet. My daughter taught him to sit on her finger and kiss her on the nose.

"That's the cutest thing I ever saw!" I exclaimed, when she showed me. "Let me get the camera." I didn't have a flash cube at the time, so I asked her to take the birdie out on the front porch. At the very moment he leaned forward to give her a peck, I skillfully snapped the picture.

I'm especially glad I got that one for our family record, because as I pressed the shutter, birdie flew away.

Come, see a man who told me everything I ever did. Could this be the Christ? (John 4:29)

I enjoy taking pictures and it's a thrill when I take an especially good one. Fortunately, I can choose which ones go in the family album, and toss out the bad ones. Unfortunately, God also records all my life "pictures," both good and bad. But He is such a merciful editor. When I tell him I regret being caught in that pose, he graciously tosses out the ugly picture—and he even destroys the negative.

As far as the east is from the west, so far has he removed our transgressions from us. (Ps. 103:12)

Who's Got My Pickle?

"When do we get lunch?" my husband asked as soon as Joanie and I came back from Saturday morning shopping.

"Soon as we can get this stuff put away," I answered. "Man, the store was crowded!"

I began to pull forty dollars worth of groceries out of two sacks. "Rats," I muttered. "I was going to make toasted cheese sandwiches for lunch, but I can't find the cheese I just bought."

"You probably lost it," my husband said cheerfully, "after you paid for it."

"I did not! I watch the checker."

"Maybe you just thought you bought it."

I glared at him. "I *know* I bought that cheese. I distinctly remember because I was going to get a chunk of longhorn for $2.85, but then I remembered you liked cheddar the best, so I found a piece for $2.25, and tossed it in the basket on top of the canned ham."

"I'll go look in the trunk," he offered, and went out.

Canned ham? I thought. *I didn't buy any canned ham, did I?* I looked down in both sacks. Nope, no ham.

"Guess what?" I giggled, when he came back in. "I just realized I must have put that cheese in somebody else's basket! Isn't that hilarious?"

"Just hysterical," he answered. "Now, what do we have for lunch?"

"How about a cold beef sandwich?"

"That would be okay, if we weren't out of dill pickles."

When I pulled out the last item from the sack I gasped, then swallowed a grin. I wasn't the only person who put their stuff in someone else's basket! With savoir-faire and a touch of snootiness, I placed the jar on the table.

I smiled and said, "Who says we're out of dill pickles?"

Jesus replied, "You are in error because you do not know the Scriptures or the power of God." (Matt. 22:29)

Everybody makes mistakes—and I think I make more than anyone else, and yet the dear Lord keeps fixing things up for me. How grateful I am that He "fixed up" the worst error of my life—the error of hoping that my good deeds would somehow outweigh my bad.

By the name of Jesus Christ . . . salvation is found in no one else, for there is no other name under heaven given to men by which we must be saved. (Acts 4:10–12)

Many of Those Days

I'm about half scared to go to the next Women's Missionary meeting. The Board has been a little testy with me ever since I was appointed Publicity Chairman, but now I'm afraid they'll ask me to resign. Last winter I kept missing important events because I could not seem to get it through my head that in order for an item to appear in the church newsletter it had to be turned in two weeks early. I don't know how many of the little items I composed (and some of them were very clever) ended up in File Thirteen because they were a day or two late.

The women were always nagging at me, saying things like: "Why didn't you turn in something about the missionary from Zuluville?"

"I did!" I would retort. "Only the typist refused to put it in the newsletter."

Of course, you can only say that with conviction about twice, and then you have to think of another excuse.

At the last board meeting I promised the WMS President I would be on my toes and do a good job of publicity. She looked so grateful, and gave me a list of coming events for the next two months.

"I mark my calendar ahead," she hinted wistfully.

"I'll do better than that!" I bragged. "I'll not only mark my calendar, but when I write the item I'll give the *day* of the event as well as the date. That way, people will be sure to remember."

Unfortunately, several people went to the Ice Cream Social on a Thursday night, and found a dark church; also, some ladies came to a luncheon that wasn't; and others brought old clothes to put in a box that was not there on Tuesday afternoon—

Tomorrow night is the Women's Missionary Meeting—I think. I dread to go. I don't know how to tell them that somehow my May calendar got turned back to April.

Do you see a man who speaks in haste? There is more hope for a fool than for him. (Prov. 29:20)

I know the Lord has given me a good mind—so what's my problem? Thoughtless? Careless? *Foolish.* Forgive me, Lord.

Do not be foolish. (Eph. 5:17)

Clamor Girl

Oh, to be chic and glamorous! I have this dream where I swoop into a room, head held high, stomach in, flawlessly attired, and not a hair out of place. Women seethe with envy, gentlemen leap to their feet and offer a chair, and I, like Princess Grace, smile regally, then sit down with knees together and slender feet crossed at the ankles. My gown is the latest fashion, spotless and wrinkle-free. When I speak, my voice is soft but sure, and I do not stammer or hesitate.

I try to make this dream a reality. And while I probably could never be considered glamorous, at least I try to have my hair fixed and have on clean clothes when I go out. But somehow, I always manage to arrive looking like a pup who has been playing in the rain.

Last night we went to the business meeting at church, and it began to rain. By the time we got there, all the good parking places were taken and we had to walk quite a way. I had on my best white slacks, too. It would be understandable to get a few little mud spots on the bottoms, but when we entered the brightly lit room I discovered I had a big muddy smear on my stomach.

"Let it dry," my husband advised. "Then you can brush it off."

I had to give my report before it dried. I knew everyone was looking at the mud, so I kept trying to hold pages over it, and I dropped some. When I bent down to pick them up,

I bumped heads with the moderator who had bent down to help me.

Then after the meeting I got into a discussion with the new youth leader (who is very cute). When I got home I discovered I had lipstick on one tooth.

"Does my girl feel grumpy?" my husband asked at breakfast.

I groaned.

"How can you love anybody who is so sloppy—so overweight—so—*klutzy*?" I stormed.

"It's hard." He nodded with a grin.

When I began to cry he hugged me.

"If I was all rolled up in bandages," he said, "and you couldn't see me, would you still love me?"

"Of course," I snapped. "It would still be you inside."

"Guess that answers your question." He kissed me. "I love the you *inside*."

Your beauty . . . should be that of your inner self, the unfading beauty of a gentle and quiet spirit, which is of great worth in God's sight. (1 Peter 3:3–4)

I am going to keep on trying to improve, and look as nice as I can, for my husband's sake—and for Jesus. But I'm so grateful that neither of them put me down because of my outward appearance.

Man looks at the outward appearance, but the LORD looks at the heart. (1 Sam. 16:7)

Creepy Crawlies

Last night when I opened the kitchen cupboard to get a snack I saw a flash of insect legs. I don't know what kind of bug it was, because it darted in a crack, but whatever it was, I was scared and sickened. In a way, I hope it was a spider. That would be better than a cockroach! (Unless it was a *black widow* spider!) Oh! I honestly don't know which frightens me the most. Maybe it was only a silverfish, or a forked-tail water bug—but it might have been a scorpion! Whatever it was, it almost sent me into hysterics. *I hate bugs!*

What really terrifies me is to discover a spider on the ceiling. Then I know I have to climb up on a chair and try to pick it up with a piece of Kleenex—or make a swipe at it with a broom. Either way, it usually gets loose; then I know I have an angry spider in the house, ready to get even, probably by dropping on my bed in the night.

There's no logical reason for me to be so afraid of insects. I know they have to be here to balance nature, and they have very tiny bodies—compared to a dog for example, and I'm not afraid of dogs.

Maybe the reason is because insects are so prolific. I could tolerate one spider (if he kept his distance) or one cockroach—but if I allow one to live, they soon take over.

After I saw those hairy legs scurrying away last night I

used up about half a can of insect spray. I may never know what kind of bug it was—I hope. One good thing about the ordeal, after it was over I was in no mood for a bedtime snack.

He sent swarms of flies that devoured them. . . . He gave their crops to the grasshopper, their produce to the locust. (Ps. 78:45–46)

I see a similarity between cockroaches in my cupboard, and sin in my life. Bugs take away my appetite for food; sin robs me of my appetite for the *Word.* It's too bad I'm not as frantic to get rid of sin in my life as I am insects in my kitchen.

Do not let sin reign in your mortal body. (Rom. 6:12)

Cucamonga Concert

"I have to spend this coming week all alone," I complained to my girl friend in Cucamonga. "The kids get to go to a church retreat, and my husband will be away on business." I sniffed piteously.

"Come stay with us!" she cried. An orange light flicked on as I remembered the weekend I took care of her Teeny Tots—but a whole week alone seemed pretty dismal.

"Well—maybe a couple of nights—"

"Fantastic!" she squealed. "We'll have a ball!"

Teeny Girl's bed was quite comfortable, even though she insisted I share it with her Barbie doll, Raggedy Ann, Oscar the Grouch, and Pooh Bear. I certainly wasn't lonely, but I didn't sleep too well. The furnace went on and off about every fifteen minutes, the toilet whistled softly, their poodle barked often, and the light was left on in the hall. It must have been close to five in the morning when I finally went sound asleep.

At six I was awakened by a heavy thud—it was a huge Children's Bible, dropped on my chest.

"Wood zoo wead me a story?" Teeny Boy asked as he climbed in bed and put his icy feet on my stomach.

A good while before breakfast I learned that my friend's eleven-year-old son is quite a pianist. He can really play *Saber Dance.* And he did. Over and over and over. Loudly. Later in the day I discovered he is learning to play the trumpet. Loudly. His musical accomplishments also include playing the harmonica. Loudly.

After breakfast, I learned Teeny Girl also takes piano lessons and shares her older brother's enthusiasm for music. She or the brother played the piano most of the day, with Teeny Boy adding a few licks from time to time.

"I get a little tired of it sometimes," my friend shouted, "but they all love the piano so much I hate to discourage them." She smiled indulgently at Teeny Boy. "I think this little one also has talent," she observed, as he stuffed Silly Putty into the harmonica.

Because the children preferred to be indoors, near the piano, we didn't get to visit much through the day. I was looking forward to the time when they would go to bed and we could start "having a ball." But *Jesus of Nazareth* was on TV that night, and naturally, all three wanted to see it. (Not hear it, because they giggled and quarreled all through it.) When it was over I stumbled off to bed, and the kids were still wide awake.

At 2:00 A.M. I awoke to the sound of the piano. I sat up straight. *Those kids surely do love the piano,* I thought. I slipped out of bed and peeked into the living room. The cat was strolling up and down the keyboard. My friend stretched and yawned into the living room.

"Cat wants out," she mumbled.

With a final plink the cat jumped off the piano and strutted to the front door. *I don't believe this,* I thought, as I stumbled back to bed.

I was exhausted, but contented, when I drove into our garage the next day. There is absolutely no place like home.

Lord, you have assigned me my portion and my cup; You have made my lot secure. The boundary lines have fallen for me in pleasant places. (Ps. 16:5–6)

We aren't rich. But how pleasant, how peaceful, how private, our home is! Thank You, Lord.

He restores my soul. (Ps. 23:3)

 May

Cover Up

My son Ron's Mother's Day gift to me was "wrapped loose." That is, it was still in the paper bag from the store! He apologized, but I thought it was fine. Why should he spend more money for pretty paper and a bow?

Gift wrapping is stupid. I wonder how the custom got started? Maybe some caveman on his way to a birthday party didn't have anything to give his friend but an old bone, so he wrapped it up pretty, in fur skin, with maybe a banana on top, in hopes he could have his piece of the dinosaur cake before they saw his moldy bone.

However it got started, it seems a waste of time and money. What advantage is there to gift wrapping? Probably wedding receptions wouldn't be as pretty if all the gifts were piled on the tables in brown paper bags and cartons, but it would help the bride and groom sort out duplicates.

One reason the Christmas season is so hard is because of all the gift wrapping. It's bad enough to shop and pay for all those gifts—why do we have to wrap them? If we would all be brave enough to quit it, a lot of messy work, time, and money would be eliminated at Christ*mess*time.

Gift wrapping isn't easy. One of my friends whose parents have divorced and remarried, had to wrap Mother's Day gifts for her mother, stepmother, mother-in-law, and three grandmothers! She was fit to be *tied!*

And it is so expensive. The paper is beautiful, and the

bows and tie-ons are precious. But what happens when you present your gift? *Rip! Slash! Wad! Trash.* Approximately a dollar tossed away. Some department stores used to gift wrap, but now it costs as much as *five dollars* to hide what the giver gives to the gift-ee.

So, I'm glad Ron had sense enough just to give me the gift. In fact, I think I'll ask him if he would like to be a charter member of a club I might start—the BGO Club (Bare Gifts Only). Our meetings would be a time to get together and (w)rap. We could *bow* our necks against this paper custom. We could even *rib*bon another. And of course, there would be no strings attached. I guess that about wraps it up.

The gift of God is eternal life in Christ Jesus our Lord. (Rom. 6:23)

When I try to explain to people that salvation is a free gift of God, do I wrap it up in so many layers of tradition, doctrine, and dogma that they never find the Gift?

Thanks be to God for his indescribable gift! (2 Cor. 9:15)

Memorial Fray

We spent Memorial Day with my mother-in-law, so that my husband and his brother could put up a patio for her. I love my in-laws, and they are good to me. But for some reason I always do something especially foolish when I'm with them—like pouring coffee on the table, or stopping up the kitchen drain, or bringing a half-baked chicken to a family potluck. I was determined this day to be on guard, and make my husband proud of me.

We women sat around drinking coffee, and watching the fellows work, and by lunch, concentrating all the while, I hadn't done anything too peculiar.

After lunch, when the fellows went back to work, my sister-in-law, Pat, asked if I would like to go with them to put flowers on the family graves. Although a cemetery is not a fun place, it was Memorial Day, and I was honored to think she wanted to share this personal time with me.

At the cemetery, Pat asked me to get some water for the containers. I grabbed the water can, eager to be of service, and loped off toward a far-away hose.

"Come back!" she called, and pointed to a faucet that stood out like a fire hydrant only a few feet away.

I got the water, then squatted down beside her to help pull crab grass off the headstones. I was yanking up grass like a starved cow when I became aware of intense pain in my ankles. I thought it was the position I was in, so I got on

71

my knees, but my ankles still hurt, and my hands began to sting. Suddenly I realized I was covered with tiny brown ants. I leaped up, stamping and shouting. But it was too late. Those tiny tyrants had even infiltrated my slacks.

Because Pat and Mom were both working away as though nothing had happened, I tried to calm down and behave in a way that honors the dead. I helped arrange the flowers, but it is very difficult to act dignified when you have first-hand knowledge that there were ants in the plants!

I don't know what the people across the road thought as they watched me squirm and stamp. I wonder, too, what *they* thought, up there. If they can look down, I imagine my father-in-law, if he is anything like my husband, was on his cloud, rolling with laughter.

We are always confident and know that as long as we are at home in the body we are away from the Lord. We are confident, I say, and would prefer to be away from the body and at home with the Lord. (2 Cor. 5:6, 8)

It is some comfort for us to put flowers on our loved ones' graves, to show we have not forgotten. But the greatest comfort is the sure knowledge that *they are not there.* They are with the Lord.

He is not here: He has risen. (Matt. 28:6)

Decorating Decorum

I shouldn't brag about my decorating, but I must say that I am artistic. It's just that some of my ideas are a little unique.

For example, a couple of years ago the women of the church asked me to decorate for the Christmas party. I got a wonderful idea, in a department store. They had gigantic golden ornaments, with tiny mirrors glued on them, twirling lazily from the ceiling. They were gorgeous, but of course our Women's Missionary Society couldn't afford anything like that. So I got the idea of buying gigantic balloons, spray painting them gold, then rolling them in glitter. There were ten of them and I hung them from the beams in the Fellowship Hall. With sparkling garlands draped around the room, and our "gold ornaments" turning in the air current, the hall was almost as breathtaking as the department store.

During dinner I noticed one of the balloons had shriveled like a grape. By game time three more had turned to golden raisins. Humiliated, I watched all but one gasp and die. During the devotion the last ornament expired with a fluttery raspberry.

So, I didn't take offense when the missionary president cautioned me, "No balloons for the Mother-Daughter banquet."

The theme was "Far Above Rubies" from Proverbs 31. I immediately visualized snow-white tablecloths, red flowers, white clouds, and rubies. I could spray paint rocks with red enamel and sprinkle them with glitter to make rubies, but what could I use for clouds?

Certainly not plain old cotton.

The night of the banquet the tables were spectacular! Each had a red carnation centerpiece, and sparkling "rubies" were strewn liberally up and down, resting on clouds of gossamery spun glass, furnished by a local insulator. With clasped hands, I had to admit I had outdone myself.

Halfway through dinner several ladies began to scratch. The woman across from me sneezed over and over. Eyes were running, welts appeared on faces and arms, little girls cried, and mothers were angry. One dear old lady claimed she had spun glass stuck in her gums.

Fortunately, nobody sued the church, but I doubt they'll call on me again.

Pity too, because I have a whole sackful of chicken feathers I'm sure I could work into this year's theme.

Be very careful, then, how you live—not as unwise, but as wise, making the most of every opportunity. (Eph. 5:15–16)

Oh how I wish my zeal in decorating had been coupled with practical knowledge! Only God knows if someone there that night was ready to receive Christ, only to be turned off by discomfort.

Do not be wise in your own eyes. (Prov. 3:7)

A Pox on Locks

One thing I'm looking forward to in heaven is that there won't be any *locks*. I've had problems with keys and locks ever since I was in junior high and couldn't remember the combination to my locker.

No doubt I've inherited this lock-resisting trait from my dad who always left the keys in our old Chevy. None of us carried a house key because our home was never locked. We lived in a small town and everyone knew we didn't have anything worth stealing.

"It's different here," my husband warned. *"Always* keep the doors locked—you never know what lunatic is around."

During our marriage I've probably broken all records for locking myself out. I do real well for a while, and then when I'm least expecting it, I accidentally slam the door with the night lock on, or forget to take the keys. All our screens have little holes in them where I've had to put a nail file or screw driver through to unlatch them.

"I don't see why you're so upset," I said when my husband began to utter strange noises. "It's just a little hole."

Once I even broke a pane of glass in the back door so I could reach in and unlock the knob.

House locks aren't the only kind I have problems with. It was just last spring when I left the keys in the car and locked mother and me out at the market, and it was raining. I hustled her and our basket of groceries back in the store while I ran around trying to find someone with coat hanger experience. The fellow who helped me messed up the rubber molding on the window, but anyway, we got in.

"At least I didn't break a window!" I yelled when my husband was crabbing about the damage.

He was really crabby yesterday when I called him at work. "Honey," I began, "you won't believe this—"

"Yeah, I will," he said. "What's wrong?"

"I just put five sacks of groceries in the trunk of the car, okay? And without thinking I put my purse in, too—and as soon as I slammed the lid I realized the keys—"

"Where are you?" He sounded tired.

After I told him, I said meekly, "And-uh—hurry, if you can. There's ice cream—"

I'm so glad that in heaven I won't have to worry about the keys—Peter will.

On no day will [heaven's] gates ever be shut, for there will be no night there. (Rev. 21:25)

Just think, in heaven there will be no sorrow, no sickness, no pain. No locks, no keys, no strain! No wonder I'm looking forward to eternity.

[Jesus said] I will give you [Peter] the keys of the kingdom of heaven. (Matt. 16:19)

Chess, Anyone?

We went to Radio Shack the other night, and while my husband looked at CBs I looked at a calculator—or was it a computer? I get those two words mixed up. The thing I looked at was sort of like a TV on top of a typewriter. It was on, and there were white words flickering on a gray screen. The message read:

HI! I LIKE TO PLAY CHESS. WOULD YOU LIKE TO PLAY CHESS? IF SO, MAKE YOUR MOVES BY SELECTING A NUMBER AND A LETTER. WHEN YOU ARE READY TO PLAY, PUSH THE 'ENTER' KEY.

I looked around shyly to see if anyone was watching. The salesmen were busy with customers. I looked at the thing again. Evidently it was eager to play. I don't know how to play chess, but it seemed a shame to disappoint the little gork. Timidly, I pushed the 'ENTER' key, and marveled at the amazing instrument.

Immediately the words vanished and a checker board began to appear, row by row. The rows across were designated A to H, and the columns down were numbered. When the design was finished, two words appeared at the bottom of the screen:

YOUR PLAY. (Fantastic!)

How should I start? It was a checkerboard, so chess must be similar, I reasoned. I typed, "A-6," and the thing answered: PUSH ENTER KEY.

I did.

77

The board disappeared! Had I broken it? Then one word leaped out for the whole store to see: ILLEGAL.

Frantically I jabbed the ENTER key, but the word ILLEGAL stayed. I poked some other keys, but nothing would erase that sinful word. I looked around. The salesmen were still busy, and my husband was grinning at a speaker that rasped out, 'Break, twenty-one." Nonchalantly I moved over to him.

He said, "Next payday let's buy a CB."

They'll probably have gork repaired by next payday. I wonder if I can learn to play chess by then?

Even so, when you see all these things, you know that it is near. (Matt. 24:33)

The Lord must be pleased when His creatures use the brains He gives them and invent amazing things like the computer. But there are so many fantastic inventions, so many brilliant innovations today, I wonder if we are nearing the time of the end!

I praise you because I am fearfully and wonderfully made. (Ps. 139:14)

Uh, Well—No

A casual acquaintance invited me to a jewelry party the other night. I wanted to say *no* for three reasons: I hate to leave my husband; I don't like to drive at night; and I couldn't afford to buy any of the stuff. But this lady is formidable. I was afraid she would be upset if I said no.

When I left home I was running late—probably a subconscious desire to stay home. I wouldn't look at the speedometer as I floor-boarded along, because if I was speeding I didn't want to know about it. If I made all the lights, I would only be about fifteen minutes late. I reached for my purse to get a breathmint, and my stomach dropped. I had left my purse at home.

"Rats!" I exclaimed. "I can't buy anything without the checkbook!" But, that would be a good excuse not to buy. Then I realized I didn't have my driver's license, either. I didn't want to break the law, so I made a quick U in the middle of the block and raced for home.

Just as I got within a block of the railroad tracks I saw the guard things come down, and the bell began to ring.

"Oh no!" I wailed. But I wasn't going to be outfoxed by a train. I made a squealing right and sped down a street parallel to the tracks. When I thought I had gone far enough to outrun the train, I turned left and rushed down the dark street. A chain link fence gleamed in the headlights.

"Dead end!" I squalled.

Tires screamed as I made another U, roared back up the street to the parallel street I had been on in the first place. By this time cars were lined up for a block, and the train stretched across the intersection like a dead boa constrictor. After I waited five minutes in line, the train hadn't even shuddered. Forty-five minutes late. I decided to turn out and find a telephone, but suddenly the snakey-freight bucked, groaned, and came alive. Box cars rumbled by. I could see the caboose! Then brakes screeched. The train faltered, then halted. I gasped! It was moving backwards! I couldn't *stand* it.

When I walked in the front door I had already taken off my shoes.

"Short party?" my husband asked. I smiled and let my stomach relax.

"Long train." I went to the phone and dialed. "I hope you won't be upset, but I can't come to the party."

Instead of wasting gas, violating traffic rules, and putting myself through an obstacle course, why hadn't I said *no* in the first place?

If you have been trapped by what you said ... then do this ... to free yourself. Go and humble yourself; press your plea. (Prov. 6:2–3)

I must learn to sort out my motives. It's one thing to say *yes,* when I know it is the Lord telling me; but I have to be on guard, and strong enough to say *no* when I am being pressured by people—or worse, by my own ego.

Modulating Seatcover

One Friday afternoon my husband called from work.

"I got my check," he said. "Let's go to Radio Shack tonight and buy that CB I was looking at."

I had hoped he would get over that notion, because I wanted to spend the money on new curtains for the bedroom. But I guess he deserves a new toy now and then. Besides, I thought, if I let him get the CB he won't dare give me any problem about getting the curtains next payday.

He spent most of Saturday installing our Citizens Band Radio in his pickup truck, while I read the CB lingo to him.

"Did you know women are called better halves, seatcovers, and beavers?" I snorted. "How gross! You better not call me a beaver." I looked over at him. "Better half, maybe." His attention was completely focused on screwing a metal plate underneath the instrument panel.

"Modulating means talking," I read on. "Police are bears; ten-twenty is your location; ten-four means okay; sixes and eights are good numbers—do you have to talk like this when you use it?"

"Ten-four," he answered.

After much frenzied drilling, grunting, and panting, he had the CB ready to test. We backed out of the driveway and on to the street before he turned it on.

"Good grief!" I yelled over the horrible, nerve-wracking static. "Does it always sound like this?"

81

"I'm trying to squelch it!" he yelled back.

I put my fingers in my ears, but I could still hear the shattering, cracking static. No amount of dial-turning helped. At last he clicked it off. He looked sad and pitiful as we drove back to Radio Shack. I'm sure he was thinking of all the money he had spent. I *know* that's what I was thinking.

The clerk smiled.

"No problem! You just need to get your whip clipped to fit." (Which being interpreted is, the antenna had to be adjusted to the proper wave length.) So, after more money and a clipped whip we were CB people again.

Now I have a problem. Next payday he wants to buy a CB for the family car, so that if we should ever be driving both cars we can talk to one another. But I still want bedroom curtains. I wonder if he would settle for a couple of walkie-talkies?

May the words of my mouth and the meditation of my heart be pleasing in your sight, O Lord, my Rock and my Redeemer. (Ps. 19:14)

I'm not sure I want a CB. My mouth gets me into enough trouble just within the circle of family and church friends. What might happen if my words go wafting out on air waves? On the other hand, I could tell the whole world about Jesus—well, at least the people in the next block.

June

My Country

One of the kids asked me to write a patriotic skit they could put on at school. Not daunted by the fact I know nothing about playwriting, this is what I wrote.

FLAG DAY

Cast of Characters:

George Washington	Patrick Henry
Christopher Columbus	Betsy Ross
William Braddock	Nathan Hale
Rev. John Eliot	Abraham Lincoln
Benjamin Franklin	Paul Revere

Scene: Airport in Heaven
Props: Clouds and a Golden Chariot

George: It was good of HIM to let us go down for a visit on Flag Day.

Christopher: It sure was. I'm anxious to see if I recognize any of the New England States. Hey! There's Governor Braddock and some of the Pilgrim Fathers.

William: Gentlemen! We've just been wondering if our heirs still have the right to worship the Lord. I'll never forget our first Thanksgiving. You weren't with us yet, were you Reverend Eliot?

85

John:	No. My work came later with the Indians. I fervently pray they are all Christians by now. Why, Benjamin Franklin! Are you coming, too?
Benjamin:	Wouldn't miss it! Tell me, George, do you know if they are still using the same old Constitution?
George:	Oh yes—but they keep amending it. I say, isn't that Pat Henry? And Betsy and Nathan—bless his young heart! Ho, everyone! Are you ready? Let's get on board this golden chariot. We're supposed to pick up Mr. Lincoln and Paul Revere on Cloud Nine.

Curtain—scene changes to earth

George:	Well, there's the old Delaware, but I would never have recognized it, if HE hadn't given me this map.
Chris:	I don't see one familiar landmark. Of course, there was nothing but beauty here in 1492.
William:	Fortunately I see hundreds, yea, thousands of churches!
John:	But—if the people who attend them really believe in Christ, how could they crowd the Indians into that little space on the worst land?
Benjamin:	Isn't this supposed to be Flag Day? Do any of you see a flag?

Patrick:	Not one! I'm glad I don't live there anymore. I think they've let the bloody communists take control. I said it before and I say it again: 'Give me liberty or give me death!'
Betsy:	I certainly would not have stuck my fingers to the bone making that flag if they weren't going to use it—and definitely would not have cut up that gorgeous red satin petticoat.
Paul:	This? This is what I risked my life for that night? I thought I would be killed any moment. And these people today couldn't care less.
Nathan:	I'm disgusted. I'm glad now I only had one life to give for this country. Even that was a waste.
George:	Jove. I'm almost sorry to be the Father of this mess.
Abraham:	Hold on, men—uh, and Ms. Ross. Look carefully! There are *some* flags waving. See, by the post office? And one yonder, by those golden arches? And a small one there by that little cottage—
George:	By Jove, Brother Lincoln, you're right!
Abraham:	Surely, those soldiers at Gettysburg did not die in vain. Perhaps even yet this nation will have a new birth of freedom, and that government of the people, by the people, for the people, shall not perish from the earth.

End.

Everyone must submit himself to the governing authorities, for there is no authority except that which God has established. (Rom. 13:1)

I haven't heard whether or not they'll use my play. I'm sure it would never win an Academy Award. But great writers say to write what you feel, and I feel intensely about the United States. I want us Americans to get the sleep out of our eyes and see what we've got, and to be proud enough and grateful enough to hang out the flag—at least on Flag Day.

We will . . . lift up our banners in the name of our God. (Ps. 20:5)

Happy Father's Day

"What can I get you for Father's Day?" I asked my husband.

"Nothing," he answered with a smile. "I'm not *your* father."

"Yes, but you bought me that expensive Chantilly perfume and bath powder set for Mother's Day!"

"That's different. Besides, if I need anything I can always get it."

"Oh, come on—I want to get you something. The kids never get you very much."

"Okay—if it will make you happy, let's go down to the hardware store and browse around. I may see some little thing you can get me."

In the hardware store we wandered up and down the aisles, looking at nails, screws, electric cord, and string. In the plumbing section he handled a couple of plumber's tools, examined some toilet replacements, turned a chrome faucet. I tried to appear interested while he watched an automatic slide show about the virtues of some varnish. In the automotive section I watched alertly as he fingered windshield wipers, pumped up a hydraulic jack, and counted wrenches in a plastic bag.

When he turned toward the power tools I went the other way. Those things cost a lot more than the amount I could spend.

89

"Look at this!" he called after me. I walked back and stood beside him. "This workbench is on sale! I've always wanted one!"

I looked at the price—that was on sale?

He was twisting bolts and twirling things, making the table part slide back and forth. He was grinning and rubbing the wood. There was no point in fighting. This was what he wanted. I took a quick peek at our checkbook. If I put off the car insurance until the following payday—he was walking away!

"Hey! Where you going?" I trotted after him.

"Too much," he said pleasantly.

I thought of all the things he did for me, the kids—my whole family; how hard he worked, what a good man!

"Not too much!" I said firmly. "Happy Father's Day!"

In the Lord, however, woman is not independent of man, nor is man independent of woman. For as woman came from man, so also man is born of woman. But everything comes from God. (1 Cor. 11:11–12)

I'm so thankful, Lord, that *this* man is the head of our house.

Honor your father ... that it may go well with you. (Eph. 6:2–3)

Hair

I could not believe how much my husband paid the other day to have his hair shampooed, cut, and blown dry.

"By a cute blonde, too," he teased.

"I have never paid that much," I retorted. "You must have given her a big tip!"

He raised his eyebrows and rolled his eyes.

I walked all the way around him. "It doesn't even look that good," I scoffed. "I'll bet I could do just as well."

He didn't answer as he walked into the living room.

"I ought to take a barber course," I called after him. "I could almost pay for it with what you spent on that haircut."

"That would be great," he called back. "Even though that lady barber was cute, it takes a lot of time to get a haircut, to say nothing of the money."

"I'll bet I could do as well as she did *without* taking a course! What do you think about me getting a barber kit?"

"Well—" There was a long pause. "Maybe you could give me a trim."

I bought the set and when his hair was beginning to look a little shaggy I coaxed him on to the kitchen stool, plugged in the new clippers, and began.

He was *so* nervous and fidgety. I can't imagine what his problem was.

"I've *read* the *instructions*," I told him, and I had, sort of, but he had no confidence in me whatsoever. I began to get nervous myself, and unfortunately, I did clip it pretty high and thin behind his right ear. Those clippers move faster than a speeding bullet. I tried to pat some of the clippings back on that spot, but as soon as he held up the mirror to look, it all fell off.

He was deathly quiet. There was so much silence in the kitchen I could hear the electric clock in the front room.

When he came back from the barber shop there was a thin, high spot behind his *left* ear, and I started to tell him that *I* could have done that. He didn't seem to be in a mood to talk though, so I kept silent. At least it looked even in the back. It was bald all the way across.

I don't know if I'll enroll in a haircutting class or not, but I have about six weeks to make up my mind. It will take at least that long for him to quit looking like Kojak.

Pride only breeds quarrels, but wisdom is found in those who take advice. (Prov. 13:10)

What made me think I could cut my husband's hair without first learning how? Too much confidence in my ability is plain old arrogance—and has gotten me into a lot of trouble. Am I also spiritually arrogant? Do I clip and cut people by spouting Scriptures before I learn *all* the Bible teaches on the subject?

I hate pride and arrogance. (Prov. 8:13)

Paper Habit

Just as an alcoholic lives in fear of running out of liquor, I live in fear of running out of paper products. When I yank that last sheet of ScotTowel off the roll, and there's no more in the pantry, withdrawal symptoms begin. What did people do before paper towels were invented? What did they do when they dropped an egg on the floor? I don't know of any way to clean up a raw egg without paper towels—unless I can get the dog to slurp it up. And then, if there's a spill on the carpet, how else can I clean that up without paper towels? Of course, I could use paper napkins, but it's practically the same thing. Woe unto me if I'm out of both at the same time.

Even worse is to be out of Kleenex, especially if you have a cold. Have you tried to use a cloth hanky lately? It feels as though you're rubbing your nose with an emery board. At home you can always use toilet tissue, but it's embarrassing to pull out a length of Charmin in public.

Absolutely the worst thing that can happen is to run out of all paper products two days before payday. The only thing you can do then is get down the Christmas stuff and see if you can find some white tissue paper. We've run out of toilet tissue so often at our house we've even used up the crumpled tissue inside the shoe boxes.

This payday I think I'll buy a whole lot of paper products and hide them. I'll put some under the bed, some in the linen closet, and some in the attic. Then I can relax. I won't have to be afraid of running out.

Man is destined to die once, and after that to face judgment. (Heb. 9:27)

It doesn't take any more grocery money to buy a month's supply of paper than it does to buy a roll or two at a time. When will I learn I don't have to go through the anxiety of running out? (Thank You, Lord, for showing me the way to heaven before my *time* runs out.)

There will be weeping and gnashing of teeth. (Matt. 25:30)

Green Scene

All my friends have lots of plants in their homes, but I have never wanted plants. Maybe the reason is that when I was little I used to stay all night with my aunt Pauline a lot, and she had scraggly plants everywhere. She was always trying to root something in glasses of water around the sink, and in the bedroom where I slept she had three shelves in front of the window, crowded with anemic geraniums. They were in tin cans that still had their labels. Gnats were always flying around too, and I felt itchy all the time I was there. But after having lunch at my friend's house awhile back, I changed my mind about plants.

Rhea has an elegant home, and everywhere you look there is a beautiful hanging plant—ferns in elaborate mac-ramé holders, ivy in ceramic pots, philodendron in straw baskets. All of them are green and glistening. When I went home that day she gave me starters for at least ten different species.

"Be sure and talk to my babies," she said as she threw them a kiss. I also stopped at the nursery and bought more plants, some fancy leaf spray, and plant food. (I hope my husband doesn't ask me what I spent.)

I talked to the babies and they began to grow at first, but after about a month they began to wither and shed.

"You've probably talked their leaves off," my husband taunted.

"They need to be repotted," Rhea advised. "Their little feet need more room."

They did begin to grow again. In fact, some of them got so big and beautiful I decided to hang them up in the living room.

I forgot to ask Rhea how she waters them without getting her arms, stomach, shoes, and carpet wet. Also, I must ask her what I should do about the gnats that live in the Boston fern.

The righteous will flourish like a palm tree, they will grow like a cedar of Lebanon; planted in the house of the LORD, they will flourish in the courts of our God.... They will still bear fruit in old age, they will stay fresh and green, proclaiming, "The LORD is upright; he is my Rock." (Ps. 92:12–15)

God's design is marvelous. I can take a plant, put it in the right light, feed and water it, give it proper drainage, and it will *grow*. It is the same in my spiritual life. If I stay in the Light, drink the Water of Life, feed on the Word, and witness, I'm going to *grow*.

Grow in the grace and knowledge of our Lord and Savior Jesus Christ. (2 Peter 3:18)

All Keyed Up

It happened again this morning, and I hate myself. Recently, I have lost my keys about twice a week. You can't believe the anguish everyone in this family goes through!

"I thought you promised the Lord a long time ago you would always hang them up," Joanie said as she searched through the desk drawers.

"I did—" I moaned. I threw tea towels out on the counter. (I *knew* they wouldn't be in that drawer.) "I promised Him if He would only show me where the keys were so we wouldn't be late to Nina's wedding, I would *always* hang them on the hook as soon as I came in."

I glanced at Joanie—she knew better than to "sass" me, but I could see the reproach in her eyes.

"Well!" I frowned at her. "I did it for months! It's just lately I've gotten careless."

"They're not in the bedroom," Ron said. "Why don't you get an extra set made, Mother?"

"I did."

"Where are they?"

"Will you just go look in the car?" I snapped.

"The car's locked, Mother."

"Are you going to call Daddy again?" Joanie ventured.

"No!"

I dumped everything out of my purse for the fourth time.

"At least, I hope not."

I could feel tears forming. "Oh why—when I lose the dumb things, *why* can't it be when it's convenient, like Saturday, when there's a little extra time? Oh my no! It has to happen when I'm already late! Joan, call your friends and tell them we'll be late to pick them up for VBS."

I stepped out on the back porch and whispered, "Lord, please tell me what I did with them. If you'll just show me this time, I *promise* I'll hang them up from now on."

"Mother—" Ron called. "Why is the margarine with your flannelgraph lesson?"

I gasped, then ran to the kitchen.

Sure enough, there were my keys, on the first shelf of the refrigerator.

Whatever your lips utter you must be sure to do, because you made your vow freely to the Lord your God with your own mouth. (Deut. 23:23)

I'm more careful with my promises now. It's too easy for me to forget—but the Lord never forgets.

Fulfill your vows. (Nah. 1:15)

Open House

Friends our age who have made a lot more money than we have recently bought a luxurious home and invited us to their open house.

Soon after we arrived, our hostess led us to a huge, formal dining room where the table was loaded with exotic goodies.

"I'll bet this cost more than our groceries for a month," I whispered to my husband, as I reached for a plate. But my friend took my hand and led me to a crystal punch bowl.

"First you have to try my punch!" She dimpled. "It's my own recipe! Non-alcoholic, so don't worry!"

I took a big swallow, and thought my teeth would crumble. Sheer will power kept me from spitting it out. It tasted like grapefruit juice, equal parts of NyQuil and vinegar, with a dash of alum.

"I'll give you the recipe," she whispered. When she darted away I poured it in a potted palm. Sadly, it was a plastic plant and the strange liquid rippled around on the plastic dirt for all to see.

At the sumptuous table I filled my plate with gourmet goodies. I took a huge bite of sandwich, to get the taste of that punch out of my mouth, at the exact moment a tall, distinguished woman appeared in front of me.

"What's your connection here?" she inquired.

I tried to swallow, my head nodding up and down like a pelican in mating season, and pointed to my friend the hostess.

"Ah yewd oo uuk wi huh," I said.

The woman looked startled, nodded vaguely, and eased away.

"The reason I couldn't swallow," I told my husband on the way home, "was because I had never tasted sardines in whipped cream before."

"Wasn't that horrible!" he said.

"But wasn't their home absolutely beautiful?"

"Yes—" he agreed. "But I like ours better."

"How come?" I asked as I snuggled up to him.

"Number one, we can relax, and number two, we have a pot of beans at our house."

For we brought nothing into the world, and we can take nothing out of it. But if we have food and clothing, we will be content with that. (1 Tim. 6:7–8)

Sometimes, especially when the afternoon sunshine shows up all the scratches on the coffee table and how worn the carpet is, I feel a little jealous of our rich friends. But would I trade places with them? Or anyone? No! Besides, the Lord Jesus has built a *mansion* for me in the suburbs of heaven.

But godliness with contentment is great gain. (1 Tim. 6:6)

July

Fireworks, Flags, and Freedom

It's the Fourth of July, and my husband has just hung out the flag. It looks beautiful, and although it has more stars in it than the one we had when I was little, the rippling folds remind me of other Independence Days.

When I was eight and lived in Colorado, firecrackers were legal, so every Fourth of July, about four-thirty in the morning, you could count on being awakened by *Pop! Pop! Pop! Bang! Pip-pip-pip-pip-pip-pip* (lady fingers) and an occasional *Bal-looom!* All the kids got up early to shoot off their firecrackers. I wasn't allowed to have any.

"It's too dangerous for a little toot like you," Dad declared, when I asked to buy some. "Anyway," he added, as he lit a cigarette, "we can't afford just to burn up money."

Even though I didn't get any fireworks of my own, the Fourth was still an exciting day—almost as exciting as Christmas. I don't know why, exactly, unless it was because adults everywhere made a big thing of it. There were always parades and programs, and flags everywhere—on every house, on the main streets, and some people even put little flags on their hood ornaments. The grown-ups were proud to be Americans, and I grew up that way, too.

By noon most of the noise had subsided. "But not enough that I can take a nap," Dad grumbled. Every so often someone would find a firecracker in the rubble and there would be a nerve-wracking *Pop!* Afternoon was the time to light "snakes"—ugly little pills that erupted into revolting, snakelike ash. Afternoon was also the time to break open dud firecrackers and make piles of gunpowder—the bigger the pile the bigger the flame. No wonder so many kids got burned!

In the late afternoon, we usually went to Lakeside, a big amusement park in Denver. We would choose the best place from which to watch the fireworks show, then eat our picnic—fried chicken, potato salad, chocolate cake, and watermelon. At nine o'clock the fantastic fireworks began —brilliant, shimmering Niagara Falls, Abraham Lincoln, George Washington, and the finale, a gigantic red, white, and blue flag.

Yes, the Fourth of July was exciting when I was little, partly because of the fireworks and partly because of the flags. But I think most of the excitement was generated because of the people's attitude. There was no doubt in their minds that, under God, America was the greatest country in the world. Independent, free!

I have chosen: to loose the chains of injustice and untie the cords of the yoke, to set the oppressed free. (Isa. 58:6)

I pledge allegiance to the flag of the United States of America and to the Republic for which it stands, one nation under God, indivisible, with liberty and justice for all.

Jesus said, "If you hold to my teaching, you are really my disciples. Then you will know the truth, and the truth will set you free." (John 8:31–32)

Pool Aid

"Would you consider taking care of our pool while we're on vacation?" my neighbor asked.

"Would I!"

With the kids out of school for the summer it would be a godsend to have the privilege of swimming in a private, sparkling clean pool.

However, after having full charge of the pool for two weeks, I'm not certain it was a privilege.

The day before our neighbor left I went over, and she explained all the things I would have to do to keep the pool sparkling clean.

"Don't ever, ever, *ever* put the chlorine and acid in at the same time!" she warned.

"I won't!" I promised, bug-eyed. "What would happen?"

She screwed up her mouth, then declared, "I think the pool would explode."

She demonstrated how to test the water, by squirting a few drops of something in tubes. One tube had to be the right shade of yellow, and the other had to be an exact shade of pink.

"Now let me show you how to vacuum the pool. This should be done every other day."

Good grief, I thought. My living room doesn't get it that often.

"To vacuum, you have to hook this white hose to the

aluminum handle—but you'll burn up the pump if you don't do your hook-up under water."

I frowned.

"What's the matter?" she asked.

"I'm not sure I can hold my breath that long."

Vacuuming turned out to be the least of my problems.

One day I got too much chlorine in the pool and had to add water. I laid the hose down in the pool, turned on the water, and started to walk away. The water pressure made the hose whip back and forth like a snake. Suddenly, it leaped out of the water, spewed all over the windows next door, then attacked me. It took half an hour to polish the woman's windows, and when I got back to the pool, the water was sloshing out the deep end. I have an idea that's why my neighbor's verbenas are doing so poorly.

I didn't tell her about that, or about the windstorm and how it took me two hours to get the leaves and papers out of the pool; or the day my friend's poodle thought he could walk on water and almost drowned; or the day my son hit his head on the bottom. No sense in making her feel bad. Besides, she might not ask me again next year.

Whoever believes in me . . . streams of living water will flow from within him. (John 7:38)

Water is *wonderful!* Nothing satisfies thirst like a cool drink of water. No wonder we are all drawn to water. And no wonder Jesus refers to Himself as the Water of Life.

Whoever drinks the water I give him will never thirst. (John 4:14)

Ame-Fay—Shortlived

"An-kay oo-yay alk-tay ig-pay atin-lay?" the neighbor's seven-year-old girl asked.

"Ure-shay," I said, and folded my arms nonchalantly.

"Wow," she said softly. I could see I had zoomed up in her estimation. I blew on my nails and polished them on my chest.

"Besides that," I boasted, "I can write shorthand."

"Really?" Her eyes were almost worshipful. "Wait right here 'til I get my friends!"

While I waited I sang to myself—"I feel pretty, and witty and bright!" In a few minutes she returned with a boy whose arm was in a cast and a little girl with tangled hair and big glasses.

The neighbor's girl pushed them aside and said, "Would you say something to them in Pig Latin?"

"Of course," I said magnanimously, and assumed a theatrical stance. "Or-fay Od-gay o-say oved-lay ee-thay orld-way, at-thay Ee-hay aiv-gay Is-ay only-lay On-say, at-thay oosoever-hay elieveth-bay in-ay Im-hay ood-shay ot-nay erish-pay ut-bay ave-hay ever-ay-astinglay ife-lay."

All three kids stared up at me with round eyes and open mouths. After a moment of admiring silence, the neighbor's girl folded her arms and strugged back and forth before the other two.

"Didn't I tell you? Besides *that*," she spat out, *"she* can write shorthand!"

"Let's see you do it," the boy said. "You can write on my cast." I shrugged modestly, took his ball point and wrote:

They all examined it.

The boy said, "Man—can I have your autograph?"

I signed my name with a flourish.

The other little girl was silent. At last she pushed her glasses up on her nose and said,

"My married sister can *speak* shorthand."

Without a backward glance they all sped off to the sister's house.

Audiences today are pretty fickle.

For who makes you different from anyone else? What do you have that you did not receive? And if you did receive it, why do you boast as though you did not? (1 Cor. 4:7)

I love to be complimented, but it isn't good for me to be praised too much. I get to thinking *I am something,* and forget to give God the glory.

Set your hearts on things above. (Col. 3:1)

Model Kitchen

When my husband came home night before last I asked him if we could eat out.

"How come?" he asked.

"Just because," I said as I looked up into his eyes. I was too embarrassed to tell him the reason.

Usually I only wear my glasses to read, but for some dumb reason I wore them into the kitchen that afternoon to start dinner. What a revelation!

The first thing I noticed was a scuzzy look in the corners of the sink and around the faucets. It looked yukky, as though it had been sprayed with artificial snow and green paint at the same time.

I couldn't stand to look at it, much less make a salad there, so I went to the pantry to see what I could fix from cans. A couple of months back I remembered spilling a little flour, and I cleaned it up—I thought. But with my glasses on I realized everything had a film of white dust. And all this time I thought they weren't making labels as bright as they used to.

I dusted off a can of beans and a can of tomato sauce and decided to make chili and tacos for dinner. When I opened the refrigerator to get hamburger, with my glasses on, I was horrified at the meat tray. The little things I thought were chips in the porcelain were bits of mold! I picked up the package of hamburger with thumb and

109

forefinger, then took the tray out in the yard and turned the hose on it. I didn't want that thing to touch the rest of the food until I sterilized it. When I opened the crisper for lettuce I jumped when I saw something move, but it was only a very old, gray-green pepper succumbing to gravity.

I turned on the oven to keep the taco shells hot, and when I saw the dark, sticky mess in the bottom of the oven, I decided I did not want to eat anything prepared in this kitchen.

That night, after we left the restaurant, we stopped at the store for lime remover, ammonia, disinfectant, bleach, and oven cleaner, and I spent yesterday, with my glasses on, cleaning the kitchen.

Last night when my husband got home I looked up into his eyes and murmured, "Can we eat out again?"

"Again? How come?"

"I'm worn out from cleaning," I whined.

I don't know what excuse I'll use tonight—but I'm not about to mess up my beautiful kitchen.

Always give yourselves fully to the work of the Lord, because you know that your labor in the Lord is not in vain. (1 Cor. 15:58)

I really get sick of housework! Yet, I know the way I keep our home can either be a *plus* or a *minus* for the Lord Jesus. How can I explain to others the way to be cleansed by Christ, if I am a sloppy housekeeper?

We proclaim him ... teaching everyone ... to this end I labor. (Col. 1:28–29)

Automotive Aid

One of the discount stores had a sale last week and my husband wanted me to buy a battery they had advertised.

When I got to the Automotive Department the salesman was busy with another customer, and it was quite a while before he came to me. I showed him the battery ad I cut out of the paper.

"Those batteries haven't come down from stock yet," he said, "but if you don't mind waiting I'll go over to the warehouse and get them." He smiled. "Only take about ten minutes."

While he was gone I looked at seat covers, floor mats, filters, and tool boxes. I was reading the directions for installing windshield wipers when the department telephone began to ring.

After it rang about four times I looked around. There wasn't another salesman in sight. It kept ringing and I began to worry. It must be an important call or they would have given up by now.

Well, it was none of my business. I shrugged and went back to reading. But that might be the salesman's boss and the nice fellow might lose his job. After all, he had left his post to go get a battery for me.

I walked to the phone and spoke crisply. "Automotive Department."

"I'm calling for my husband," a breathless little voice

said, "and that tail pipe he bought just a little while ago won't fit and he wants to know if you'll take it back?"

"I don't know what to tell you. You see—"

"Oh please! It isn't hurt at all! Can't he bring it back?"

"Well, I'm sure it will be all right, but I don't—"

"Oh thank you! He'll come right over!"

When the salesman came pushing a cart loaded with batteries I realized what a strange thing I had done. I bit my lip and worried.

"Uh, I wanted to ask you something—" I cleared my throat and he unloaded batteries. "Uh, this lady—if a person buys something that doesn't fit their car, can they bring it back?"

"Sure you can, if you have your sales slip, but you won't have any trouble with this." He hoisted the battery up into my basket.

As I walked toward the parking lot I saw a young fellow loping toward the entrance with a chrome exhaust pipe in his hand. I surely hope he had his sales ticket.

If you suffer, it should not be . . . as a meddler. (1 Peter 4:15)

I see now that I was meddling, even though my motive and desire was to be a Good Samaritan. But I made one mistake. I forgot to pray first. On the way home I asked the Lord to forgive me for meddling. Also, I asked him to make the salesman exchange the fellow's exhaust pipe.

And we know that in all things God works for the good of those who love him. (Rom. 8:28)

Folly Hobby

My Cucamonga girl friend came over last Saturday and I was excitedly looking forward to just sitting around and talking with her. I made coffee and some goodies and got some snapshots ready to show.

When she and the Cuties came in, she was carrying a big sewing bag. We sat down at the dining table and as soon as I poured her coffee she took out a baby-blue thing and began to crochet as hard as she could.

"Hope you don't mind," she said without looking up, "but I'm trying to get this done for a baby shower."

"Is it a blanket?"

"Yes—I've made lots of them. I always have something started. Don't you have a hobby? Something you do with your hands?"

"No—I'm really not very good at things like that."

"Crocheting is fun! And it's easy. You should try it."

I decided not to tell her about my first experience. It was when I was still a bride. Crocheting was big that year and my Sis taught me how to make a square with little puffy things in it.

"It's called the popcorn stitch," she said. "You need seven hundred and two to make the bedspread—or, if you want, five hundred makes a tablecloth." That was in the summer. By late fall I had completed seven squares, and the popcorn was from a poor crop. None of the squares

113

was like any of the rest. In later years my daughter didn't even want them for her doll. I finally put them in a bag for the Veterans—and they never called me again.

While I was pregnant my patient sister taught me to knit. The goal was a baby sweater, but I could never remember if I was knitting or purling, so the garment had a curious texture. By the time I finished, Ronnie was too big to fit in it.

I can embroider fairly well, except for French knots, but why should I? I never see embroidered dresser scarves or tablecloths at my girl friends'—at least nothing like I have made.

Why handcrafts lack appeal for me I don't know. And yet, I feel I should do something with my hands when I have free time. If I had something ready to work on in the evenings maybe my hands wouldn't find the peanut dish so often. I think I'll call my Cucamonga girl friend and have her help me try Ch 2, SC 6 again.

A wife of noble character who can find? She selects wool and flax and works with eager hands. (Prov. 31:10, 13)

As a homemaker I work pretty hard. Don't I deserve to just *sit* sometimes? Of course. But the amazing thing about a hobby is that doing it is often more restful than *rest.* And the biggest bonus is mental satisfaction instead of bored discontent.

Absence of occupation is not rest. A mind quite vacant is a mind distressed.

—William Cowper

114

Let ME Do It

We don't eat out too often, so it was an exciting occasion for me the other night when out-of-town relatives insisted on taking us to dinner.

At the restaurant we had to wait awhile for a table, then the hostess motioned for us to follow her. We started down a long aisle between the counter and booths toward the back of the restaurant. A group of people were coming toward us on their way out, so I stepped to the left to let them pass, then proceeded.

Suddenly I realized I had led our family behind the counter. A busboy with a big pan of dishes hurried toward us, and then skidded to a stop. The waitress behind him bumped into him, and several dishes bounced out of his tray. They backed out and I apologetically continued on our way to the rear. One customer seated at the counter held out his cup for more coffee as I passed; and I looked up in time to see our hostess slap her forehead when she turned and saw where her party of six was.

After we were seated, a persistent fly began to pester us. I was embarrassed. I had recommended this place. I watched for an opportunity and when it landed, I smacked it with the big cardboard menu. I got it, too. My sweet aunt was very calm about the ice water in her lap, but I felt terrible. Evidently the waitress did too, because she grunted and sighed while she blotted the table and carpet.

We all ordered, and I can't remember what my husband got, but he wanted to put catsup on it. He kept tapping the bottle like a kitten playing with a feather.

Other people at our table wanted catsup too, and he wasn't getting anywhere, so I said, "Here! Let me do it." I grabbed the bottle, aimed it at his plate and gave it a hard pop. Half the contents ricocheted across his plate and down his white shirt. When the waitress came she grunted some more while she mopped at his shirt, and mumbled something about wishing she was back in Oklahoma.

Our relatives are still in town, and I think we should treat them to a nice meal out. But my husband refuses to take me out in public—which I think is a bad attitude on his part. After all, anyone can make a couple of mistakes!

We urge you . . . be patient with everyone. (1 Thess. 5:14)

Will I ever learn to be gentle and patient? Or will I always go through life like a zealous St. Bernard? Help me, Lord.

Patience is better than pride. (Eccl. 7:8)

August

Indemnity from Yosemite

August is a great month for vacations, but the older I get the more I realize that they don't always turn out as I had expected.

For example, we once had a family reunion at Yosemite National Park. The day we arrived there was a forest fire. Blue smoke was as thick in our campground as a first-stage smog alert. Noisy choppers dropped water for hours (God bless them) and finally got the fire put out. The evening breeze cleared out the canyon, but by nightfall my eyes began to water and I was coughing again.

Brother Don explained, "It's the campfires. You get two or three hundred campfires going, and there's bound to be a lot of smoke."

"But look around," I said. "Everyone is cooking on propane. Why do they make fires?"

"Whoever heard of camping without a fire?" he said.

"How could we roast marshmallows?" Timmy whined.

"Don't worry," Don assured me. "By bedtime the fires will die out, and then we'll breathe clean mountain air."

But after we went to bed the smoke in our tent got stronger. I buried my head in the pillow, but which is worse, to choke, or smother to death? Finally I peeked outside. True, most of the fires were out—except the one at the next tent. A couple of old boys were swapping tales and stoking their fire as though they were in the Yukon. Unfortunately, our tent was their chimney.

The next morning we moved our tent away from the old boys' camp, and then tried to decide what exciting thing to do. There are so many fun things in Yosemite—swimming in the Merced River (Ron lost his glasses the first day); taking hikes (two of the little kids got lost on the first one); riding the doubledecker buses (Joan got carsick).

But in spite of all this, it was great. It is so beautiful in Yosemite, and so restful. No house to clean or washing to do. All you have to do is fix three meals a day, haul water, explore with the little kids, and settle quarrels. And although some of those campers would have said our campground wasn't overcrowded, on the second night I found myself asking my husband to turn over—before I realized it was a man in the next tent doing the snoring!

Although we didn't get away from it all as planned, and the air wasn't quite as pure as we thought it would be, it was wonderful to camp out and see God's handiwork. It made me extra thankful, not only for the great outdoors, but for the great indoors.

Yet man is born to trouble as surely as sparks fly upward. (Job 5:7)

There have been enough disappointments in my life that I now try to be ready with Plan B in case Plan A does not work out. I also try, although not always successfully, to learn what Jesus is teaching me. One thing I have learned—there is no disappointment in Him.

Why spend money . . . and your labor on what does not satisfy? (Isa. 55:2)

Carpenter Chromosomes

I've been studying my neighbor's medical encyclopedia this morning, trying to find out why I have such a backache and headache. I haven't found what caused them, but I believe I have learned why I did what I did yesterday, and why my husband is upset with me.

It started at the beginning of summer. Everyone we know has a covered patio, except us. And of course, the weather is getting hotter and hotter.

"Don't get impatient," my husband kept saying. "One of these weekends when I don't have so much to do I'll get lumber and make us a patio."

Every weekend he either had to work, or trim the bushes, or work on the car; so yesterday I decided I could be helpful. I went out in the backyard to study the situation. If I used the neighbor's high cinderblock wall for the back of the "patio," I could attach our old green tarpaulin to a couple of uprights and then stretch it over to the wall. This would serve as a lean-to until he could build us a real patio.

I found a couple of nice two-by-fours in the garage and some five-gallon cans. I put two of the cans about eight feet out from the wall, filled them with dirt, stuck the two-by-fours in them, and nailed the tarp to the top of the boards. I anchored the tarp to the block wall with several big rocks.

It was really hard work filling the buckets with dirt, stretching the canvas, and getting the rocks up there. But by noon I had an eight-foot-square of solid shade! I made

121

a peanut butter sandwich, and sat in the shade of my patio. I pretended I was in Hawaii.

After my luau, I went to the garage and found a beautiful piece of plywood and some one-inch boards. By four o'clock I had made a table and two benches. They were pretty solid too—if you kept your feet flat on the ground. I draped fishnet on the back wall and hung up some shells and leis. It looked great! I couldn't wait until my husband and kids came home. I was really beat, but I fried chicken and made potato salad, and served dinner on *the patio.*

The kids loved it, but my husband said, "This is probably the tackiest thing you've ever done."

I began to cry, and nobody wanted to eat.

"I told you I would build a patio." he said.

"But you never did! And summer is almost over!" I blew my nose. "I'd rather saw and hammer!"

The neighbor's medical book explains that evidently I got some chromosomes that were intended for my brother. This accounts for why I love to do carpenter work.

If I can get over my backache and headache, I'll knock down that patio today. My honey promised he would leave work early and get a load of lumber on the way home.

Her husband has full confidence in her... (Prov. 31:11)

The Lord showed me in the Word that I was not helping my husband, but hurting him. I embarrassed him before his children *and* the neighbors, and I put him under pressure that he didn't need. My place is to *help* my husband, and let him lead.

She brings him good, not harm... (Prov. 31:12)

Different Strokes

Up until last weekend I thought I knew how to swim, but now I'm not sure the splashing, gulping, and gasping I do in the water can honestly be called swimming.

Our family was invited out to my brother-in-law's place, and they have a nice pool. It was the first time I had seen my husband swim in a long time, and as far as I'm concerned, he looks as good in the water as Mark Spitz. I marveled at his dive, and how fast he swam the length of the pool and back again.

I love to play in the water with the kids, and I was having a good time showing off my new suit (I lost three pounds for the occasion) and how well I could swim, when my husband took me aside.

"You could move through the water faster, love, if you'd keep your fingers together like a paddle."

Everyone was making a lot of noise and I thought he said saddle. I cupped my hands up and struck the water a few times and almost drowned. I floundered back to the side. He explained again and I paddled away.

"Kick your legs harder, hon'," he called after me.

I began to kick as hard as I could, forgot to paddle, and my head went under. I got my head above water in time to hear one of the little kids yell, "Keep your arms closer to your body!"

Another voice added, "Keep your knees stiff!"

"Keep your face in the water!" someone else piped.

I tried to obey them all, and what had started out as a fun afternoon now seemed like an attempt on my life. I was in the deep end, trying to remember to keep my hands paddling, arms close, face down, knees stiff, and legs kicking fast.

When I stubbed my toe on the bottom, I knew my old way was best—at least for me.

I can't swim fast, and I may look awkward, but at least the old strokes keep my head above the water.

Am I now trying to win the approval of men. . . ? (Gal. 1:10)

Sometimes the old way is best—even if it doesn't please everyone.

We are not trying to please men but God, who tests our hearts. (1 Thess. 2:4)

Fly, Fly Away

If there is anything I hate, it's flies. If there is even one fly in the house I cannot rest until I've smacked, squashed, and slayed him—no matter how many flower pots get knocked over in the process. Shell Strips are fine, but they don't work on the patio. I've worn my brain out trying to figure a way to have a meal outside without *them*. No matter how slyly I prepare the food, it's never more than three minutes after we're seated outside until we're invaded. If only our government had the communication system flies use, we'd never be surprised by the enemy!

"Ignore them," my husband always says. "They won't eat much."

Every time he says that I have an urge to dump potato salad on his head. I hate flies! I've tried to talk myself out of this insane drive to *kill* that comes over me when I see a fly. *After all,* I try to reason, *they're similar to bees. You don't hate bees, now do you? Why do you hate flies? . . . See the lovely gossamer wings on that fly on the edge of your plate?* G-r-r-r! Kill!

I guess I come by this feeling naturally. My Aunt Mab is also a fanatic fly-foiler, and has probably killed more flies than anyone in our family. Once, when we were camping, we were seated at the picnic table when a big fly began to buzz around her food. She picked up her table knife and sat there watching.

125

"What are you going to do with the knife?" I teased.

"I'm going to kill that fly," she grated. He hovered, then landed on the table. Suddenly, *wack!* She'd chopped off his head!

Yesterday, at the neighbor's pool, I again tried to feel charitable toward flies. I'm sure they have a purpose other than driving me insane. As I lay in the sun after a swim, a rather large fly alighted on my leg. His head was gold in the sun, and there were brilliant purple flecks on his green, iridescent back. He was actually pretty. He put his built-in straw into a drop of water on my leg. He was drinking! Right off my leg! How cute!

Just then I felt some pain there. What? Why, that little stinker just *bit* me! I *hate* flies!

If you do not let my people go, I will send swarms of flies on you. (Exod. 8:21)

It must be normal to hate flies—after all, God used them for punishment. Flies are like sins: they pollute, they sting, they are hard to get rid of, they multiply fast, and they take away your peace.

As dead flies give perfume a bad smell, so a little folly outweighs wisdom and honor. (Eccl. 10:1)

Eliminate the NegaTiVe

A relative of mine recently got a face lift, and she looks great. However, I think if I had that kind of money I would rather have my stomach lifted. I tried on bathing suits the other day and I couldn't believe it! As much as I would hate it, I may have to give up swimming. Lately I can't bear for the kids to see me in a bathing suit—much less strangers. One thing for sure—they'd never catch me in a bikini. (Of course, nobody would try either.) I asked a lady who was looking at swim suits how she kept her figure.

"By starving," she answered.

I know it's true. Even when I stay faithfully on one thousand calories a day, I gain. I guess I ought to start counting what I eat at night, too. But I think there is entirely too much emphasis on skinny bodies. Everybody wants to be thin. I blame TV. Every three or four minutes there is a commercial which shows some gorgeous, skinny girl whose waist is so tiny it looks as though she would break in two if she took a deep breath. Some are redheads, some brunettes, most are blondes—but they are all chesty, sexy, and skinny. And what are they selling? Not their bikinis. They advertise anything from men's suits to eyeshadow. Now why couldn't some nice lady in a muumuu sell eyeshadow?

All this skinny beauty depresses me and makes me hungrier than ever. The sponsors know this, so as soon as the bikini beauties go off the screen, then comes the food commercials—close-ups of thick, chocolate cake; lobster and steak; hot biscuits browning before your eyes. Pre-programmed dummy that I am, I get up and trundle out to the kitchen in search of another snack.

There has to be a solution. I can't let the sight of those scrumptious skinnies and sumptuous snacks ruin my summer—which will happen if I don't buy a suit and go swimming with the kids.

I think the solution is not a face lift—not a stomach lift, but a finger lift—one that snaps the TV off.

Do not conform any longer to the pattern of this world, but be transformed by the renewing of your mind. (Rom. 12:2)

How can I expect my mind to feed my body correctly, when *I* am feeding my mind incorrectly?

Offer your bodies as living sacrifices ... which is your spiritual worship. (Rom. 12:1)

The Giggler

If we had a dog house I would be in it. I got the giggles again at the wrong time and now my husband is mad at me. But of all the dopey things for him to do! He stood in front of the closed bedroom door, bent over, tying his shoes. I banged open the door, and he fell on his face. Only his ego was hurt, but he was mad as a hornet when I began to laugh. I really tried to quit, but the more I tried, the harder I laughed.

The last thing he said when he slammed the door behind him was: "There has to be something wrong with a person who laughs at another's pain!"

Maybe there is something wrong with me, because I usually laugh when I shouldn't. I remember when I was sixteen, our landlady died. I really liked the little woman and felt sad at her passing, but the day of her funeral I got the giggles. I sat between my mother and my girl friend, and all it took was just a twinkle in her eyes, and we both began to laugh. Not out loud, but our shoulders jiggled up and down, and we snuffled and choked. Mother kept poking me and frowning, but I couldn't stop. It was miserable. We would get control for a moment, then start in again.

Our eyes and noses were red when the funeral was over, and one sweet old lady hugged me and said, "Don't cry anymore, love. She's with the Lord."

Now I'm much older, but I still get the giggles at the

wrong time. Sometimes on Sunday, usually during the sermon, without warning I feel those laugh bubbles building up in me. My shoulders shake and my husband frowns and gives me an admonishing jab in the arm. I know he thinks I'm silly, but when the giggles attack me, I'm almost helpless. Lots of times when we argue, I burst out laughing. This makes him furious, but it usually stops the quarrel.

I do have serious times—this is one of them. I've been trying all day to form a speech to say tonight, about how sorry I was for laughing at him all sprawled out on the bedroom floor, but—hee, hee—I—hee, hee—can't—ulp—quit—ho, ho—laughing!

There is a time for everything . . . a time to weep and a time to laugh. (Eccl. 3:1–4)

A psychologist would be able to tell me why I laugh at the wrong time—maybe I am insecure, or immature. I am truly sorry when I laugh at the wrong time. But I am truly thankful I laugh much more than I cry.

A cheerful heart is good medicine. (Prov. 17:22)

Just Checking

Mary and I were shopping in the mall. She glanced over at me just as I pulled out my compact and looked at myself.

"You're not getting conceited, are you?" she kidded.

"Conceited? Why?" I ran my tongue over my teeth, then snapped the compact.

"Well—that's the second time you've looked at yourself since lunch."

"Oh." I grinned. "Just checking."

"What for?"

"To see if everything's okay. Remember that dinner I went to a couple of weeks ago?"

She nodded.

"I sat across the table from one of the company executives. He kept saying funny things that made me laugh. Later, when I went to the rest room I discovered I had a big piece of spinach stuck on my teeth."

"Oh, no!" Mary laughed. "How funny! How terribly embarrassing!"

"It was *gross!* I hated to go back to the table. Then later on, we all went to Thirty-One Flavors for a hot fudge sundae. I noticed every so often my husband would look at me intently, stick his tongue high up on his lip, then brush his mouth. He looked so silly! I couldn't imagine what was wrong with him. But on the way home he told me I had chocolate syrup under my nose."

Ignoring Mary's guffaw, I took out my compact again, looked at myself, and put it back in my purse.

"He told me," I went on, "I ought to carry a mirror and check myself every so often—so, that's all I'm doing. Checking."

And we, who with unveiled faces all reflect the Lord's glory, are being transformed into His likeness. (2 Cor. 3:18)

Wouldn't it be peculiar if I looked in the mirror, saw a piece of spinach on my teeth, yet did nothing about it?

Isn't it even more peculiar that I can read God's Word in regard to some sin in my life, yet do nothing about it?

In the image of God he created . . . male and female. (Gen. 1:27)

September

September Song

The kids went back to school this morning! Hurray! Goodie! Joy! Now I can relax and do what *I* want. I can have an extra cup of coffee in complete silence, without a sound from TV, stereo, or tape recorder. I won't have to settle any fights, or listen to them complain:

"There's nothin' to do—"

"When do we eat?"

"Where can we go today?"

At last I can get all their clothes hung up and their rooms fumigated. Oh! I'm so happy I feel poetical:

> No more house full of kids to feed
> No more bites from centipedes
> No more cuts on toes
> No more whining woes!

Tra la la la, tee dee. My heart is beating a calm seventy-eight instead of lurching every time some kid yells. And the poor cat—exhausted, sound asleep. No more neighbor kids yanking her up and hauling her around.

Oh! I can go out to lunch with a girl friend without having to go to McDonald's. I can read *Good Housekeeping* from cover to cover without having to find a Band-Aid or make Kool Aid.

This house is really quiet. No screen door banging, nobody jumping out and saying *"Boo!"* No gang of kids putting on a show in the backyard. It is almost an eerie silence.

I don't know how I'll stand this solitude.

But I'll manage!

Sons are a heritage from the LORD, children a reward from him. (Ps. 127:3)

I love my children—with all my heart. But that doesn't mean I don't get tired of everlastingly training them, cleaning them, and picking up after them. Hmmm—wonder if that's how the Lord feels about me?

As a father has compassion on his children, so the LORD has compassion. (Ps. 103:13)

Cutting Remarks

I'm so frustrated I feel like crying. There's an article in the paper I wanted to save and I can't find the scissors. It's a long piece, continued on another page, so I can't tear it out. I've got to have scissors. I hope I don't have to borrow my neighbor's again.

We own six pairs of scissors. There's the old Keencutters Mother gave me when I got married; some small pointed ones; a new pair with orange plastic handles; pinking shears; a pair of thinning scissors; and manicure scissors. And they're all lost. I've looked everywhere, including the refrigerator, but they've all disappeared.

If only I could blame somebody, but I'm the careless one. I never put anything away until everything is lost. Then I clean house frantically and get everything found and back in its place. Gradually, however, as I use things, one by one they disappear. There is a wicked voice inside me that whispers, *Just leave that. You can put it away later.*

Oh, why don't I listen to the voice of my conscience? Then I would know where the scissors are. Why can't I remember where I used them? One time I found the pointed scissors in the car. I had wrapped a gift on the way to a shower. Another time I found the Keencutters outside on the back walk. That time I wanted to cut roses and couldn't find the pruning shears. Another day I thought the pinking shears had disappeared for good. But I found

137

them not long ago, rolled up in some material I was going to cut out, only I couldn't find any straight pins for the pattern.

If I could find just one pair I would be happy. The thing that makes me the saddest is that I'm such a poor example to my children. The other day I overheard Ron instruct Joan not to loan Mother anything out of his X-Acto set because she'd lose it.

What am I going to do? At this point I would settle for the manicure scissors—it wouldn't be the first time my newspaper clipping had scalloped edges.

Oh! Joy! I just remembered—I got electric scissors for Christmas. They're still in their box.

. . . But what did I do with the box?

A fool spurns . . . discipline, but whoever heeds correction shows prudence. (Prov. 15:5)

I know my careless ways embarrass my family, and hurt the dear Lord. What will it take to make me change my ways?

You became imitators of us and of the Lord . . . and so you became a model to all the believers. (1 Thess. 1:6–7)

Chocolate Monkey

Lorene, a life-long girl friend, spent a week with us recently. About the third night she was here, she left me and my husband watching TV and went to her room. I heard her drag out her suitcases, and open and shut the lids. I could hear her muttering too, and then she opened the dresser drawers and banged them shut.

I looked at my husband and whispered, "What's her problem?"

He shrugged, and about that time she bounced back in the room with her jacket over her arm and a wild look on her face.

"Will you go with me to the store? I'm out of cigarettes."

"This late? In the rain? Why can't you go to bed and forget it?"

"If you won't go with me, I'll have to drive in this strange town alone. I've got to have a cigarette!"

"That's disgusting," I sneered. "Why don't you quit that stinky, harmful habit?"

She looked dangerous, and immediately I recognized it as the first stage of a nicotine fit.

"*You* don't know how it feels!"

"I'll bet I'd quit before I'd go out in the rain," I retorted.

"Oh yeah?" she yelled. "You're so crazy about chocolate —how would you like to quit chocolate? Forever!"

Visions of Hershey bars danced through my head. I

gulped. Almond Joys, Mounds, chocolate-covered cherries! *Mr. Goodbars* —(my favorite)—*forever?* I began to shake and she laughed fiendishly.

"See?" she taunted. "Now you know how I feel! But I'll make a deal with you! If you can give up *all* chocolate —no cocoa, no devil's food cake, no Ding Dongs—I'll quit smoking! At least, while I'm here."

She stayed three more days, and I never saw her smoke another cigarette. It didn't seem to bother her too much, either.

As for me, I felt as though someone had died. I had nail prints in my hands from clenching my fists. I wandered from room to room and always ended in the kitchen. I'm ashamed to say this, but I was glad to see her go.

"What's all that drawer-slamming out in the kitchen?" my husband yelled, after she was out of sight.

"Nothing," I screamed. I rifled through the tea towels and peeked into pots, but she must have taken it with her—and I *needed* that Mr. Goodbar!

You, then, why do you judge your brother? Or why do you look down on your brother? For we will all stand before God's judgment seat. (Rom. 14:10)

I am too quick to judge by someone's actions if she or he is a Christian or not. The things I do may not be as offensive outwardly as something others do—but I must remember, God is the Judge.

Who are you to judge. . . ? To his own master he stands or falls. (Rom. 14:4)

Hard-luck Potluck

"The church bulletin says there's going to be a potluck before the business meeting Wednesday night," my husband called from the living room. It was Sunday noon, and I was checking on dinner.

"I saw that," I said, as I slammed the oven door.

"You're supposed to bring a meat casserole, salad, and dessert."

"I know."

I stirred the gravy too hard and it sloshed on the burner.

"I'd rather not go," I called out.

"Not go? How come? The food is always great."

Not mine, I thought sadly. No matter how hard I try to be a good cook, I fail. There are a few things I do okay—like my husband's favorite, beef and noodles. And meatloaf —there's nothing to meatloaf if you follow the directions on the mix.

However . . . at the last church supper, the food committee decided we should all bring meatloaf. When I put my two shriveled lumps in beside the other fat, brown loaves I was so ashamed. I still don't know why mine got so small and old-looking. Maybe the oven thermostat wasn't working; or maybe they were exhausted from swimming in grease. It hurt when my traitorous husband selected some of the good-looking meat. Of course, the serving committee hadn't sliced my loaves, so that may have been the reason. I heard one teen-ager say, "Hey, man, look at the big meatballs!"

That night I also brought a jello salad. I have made so many runny jello salads in the past, I determined to be very careful to drain the canned pears, peaches, and pineapple until they were bone dry, and I only used about half the liquid called for. At the food table I watched people jab at it, whack at it, and try to cut it, but that salad firmly resisted all efforts.

Even the dessert I brought was awful. The cake was okay because it was a mix, but I tried to make a super good fudge frosting, and it was so hard and sugary the girls couldn't cut it. They finally peeled it off, cut the cake, and broke chunks of fudge to go with each piece.

I didn't pick up any of my dishes that night. I didn't want anyone to know what I brought.

"Well—" my husband called, "I definitely think we should be at that business meeting.

"Oh, I agree," I called back. "But I think I'll cook you some beef and noodles and we'll eat at home first."

Make every effort to add to your faith ... perseverance. (2 Peter 1:5)

I guess it is Satan who tries to make me quit. I am thankful the Lord Jesus Christ didn't get discouraged and quit before He went to the cross for my sins.

Be strong and courageous. Do not be discouraged. (Josh. 10:9)

Concealed Revealed

"There's a fellow at work I'd like to invite to dinner some night," my husband said.

"Fine," I answered. "How tall is he?"

"Tall? I don't know—what's that got to do with it?"

"Well, if he's six feet I'll have to clean off the top of the refrigerator," I explained. "Is he married?"

"Sure—does that matter?"

"Mmm, a little bit. If a strange woman is going to be here I had better clean out the medicine chest. Do they have children?"

"Man—I don't know—yeah, I think he has a boy."

"How old?"

"Why the third degree? What difference does it make?"

"A lot," I nodded wisely. "If he is near our kids' age I won't have to do anything to their rooms, but if he's older, then I'll have to clean them."

He sighed and shook his head.

"I'll try to get the information—good grief. I didn't know having a couple in for dinner would be such a problem."

"It's not really a problem. I just don't want you to be ashamed of the house. So, what night would you invite them?"

"Over a weekend."

"A Friday night?"

"I'll have to talk to him to see when they're free. Why?"

"If they come Friday evening after work, it's almost dark, and the drapes will be drawn. But if you have them on a Saturday afternoon, I'd better wash the windows."

I patted him.

"I wonder what I should serve? Which reminds me, I'd better clean the refrigerator a little bit, and straighten the pantry. I'd hate for a stranger—"

"Hold it!" my husband said. "Let's plan to take them out to a restaurant—and then later, when they get used to y—better acquainted with us, we can invite them here."

There is nothing concealed that will not be disclosed, or hidden that will not be made known. (Matt. 10:26)

When company is coming my guilty conscience turns on a floodlight and I see how dirty the house is. The Holy Spirit's floodlight is always on in my spiritual house.

He will bring to light what is hidden in darkness and will expose the motives of men's hearts. (1 Cor. 4:5)

Knot for Me

At the last Christian Women's Club a fashion consultant showed us how we could use scarfs to spruce up our wardrobe. Scarfs drift in and out of fashion all the time, and as the years have passed I've received more than my share of them for Christmas presents. I try to wear them periodically, but I always feel phony, as though I am trying to hide something. As a result, most of them are still in the box.

But this fashion consultant was so clever and looked so adorable each time she tied another scarf I decided to try again. I started with a big square of red satin.

"For an especially rakish look," the lady had said, "wear the knot high, almost under one ear." When I did that I looked as though my head wasn't on straight. I pulled the knot back under my chin, but I looked like a cowgirl who had lose her horse. I was determined to wear the thing, however, so I put the knot at the back, let the point hang down in front, and walked away from the mirror.

When I stepped outside to pick up the paper my next door neighbor asked, "Got a sore throat?"

Later, Joanie said, "Mother, scarfs look great. You just aren't used to them."

So on Wednesday night I wore a long blue scarf to prayer meeting. The consultant had showed us how to make a slip knot, and I fiddled with that thing for about five

145

minutes before I got it to work, but it really looked foxy, with the ends floating over my shoulders.

At church I had to take two aspirins before I realized my pounding headache was the result of my scarf being too tight. And then, when I got out of the car at home, I slammed the door on my scarf and almost choked to death before my husband could unlock the car.

"We call this one 'the butterfly,'" I remembered fashion lady saying, as she gathered a flowered square in the center and pinned it to her dress. "See how the 'wings' spread out from the brooch?"

When I tried that, the 'wings' did not spread out, but curled tightly around the pin like a cocoon.

That did it. I don't have that touch of style some women have. No matter what I do with scarfs I look as if I'm trying to "put on the dog." So, I'll put them back in the box— maybe I'll give them away as Christmas presents.

On the outside you appear ... as righteous but on the inside you are full of hypocrisy and wickedness. (Matt. 23:28)

I admire women who can wear a scarf and look as though it is a planned part of their costume. Although I can't get the hang of it, I did learn something spiritual from the experience. I can't tie something on the outside of my Christian life, either, and expect it to seem genuine unless it is genuine on the inside.

They do not practice what they preach. (Matt. 23:3)

All Mixed Up

Dear Sis,

Thought I'd take a minute to write you before I get started on the day's work. I plan to clean out the dresser drawers today, and I'm not going to let anything get me sidetracked like the last time. I didn't tell you about that day—I was sort of embarrassed for even you to know.

It started with two old boxes of Coty face powder Mother gave me. I couldn't use either one because they were the wrong shades—suntan and pink; so I decided to mix them. I poured them back and forth like a Bromo Seltzer and the next thing I knew the whole house was fogging with dust. It took about half an hour to dust everything and get back to cleaning drawers.

Would you believe I had twelve half-used bottles of nail polish? I decided to combine them, and as I look back I realize I would have saved a lot of time if I had just thrown them away. In the first place, you can't just pour nail polish in another polish bottle.

The thick goo plopped and blobbed all over my fingers, and even though I mopped as quickly as I could, there is a big, dull spot on the dresser top. Another thing, in case you ever decide to mix nail polish, put the same brands together. I found out too late that some act like vinegar and oil, and I had to throw those away—actually, I ended up by throwing it all away.

There were also about twenty old tubes of lipstick in the drawer, most of them all but used up, so I took a bobby pin and dug out the stubs and put them in a little pie pan and melted them. While they were melting I wrapped foil around a pencil, made some tubes and put them in the empty lipstick cases. I stood them up, assembly line fashion, and poured in the melted lipstick.

I figured as soon as the lipstick hardened I could peel off the foil like a candy bar, but by the time I finished pouring, the stuff had disappeared. I discovered a pool of red liquid, mixed with fuzz and boiled-over oatmeal, in the catch pan under the burners. In fact, there was a lot of lipstick in a lot of places in the area, so it took a good part of the day to clean the stove, floor, and my hands. Before I was through it was time to start dinner and I never did get the drawers cleaned out.

Experience is the best teacher, and as soon as I finish this letter, I am going to *finish* what I started.

Me

P.S. What do you think about taking half a container of aqua blue eyeshadow and a little dab of purple—don't you think they'd be lovely mixed together?

I have set you an example that you should do as I have done. (John 13:15)

I know it is Satan who presents procrastinating ideas, but I don't have to follow his lead. LORD, help me to finish my tasks today, both physical and spiritual.

Jesus said, "It is finished." (John 19:30)

October

Football Frustration

This fall I'm determined to learn football. Every year I watch games with my family, and I'm the only one who never knows where the ball is, or what down it is.

The other night the Rams were playing the Denver Broncos and I asked, "Why did that fellow run from behind those men?"

No answer.

"Darling! Yoo, hoo! I asked you a question."

"Huh?" He shot me a quick look. "Oh—he had to get ready to throw a pass—" His attention was back on the game.

"I'm sure, if I really try, maybe I can understand," I said. But there was no answer. For several minutes I watched carefully, but the players were doing the same things I've seen them do for years.

First, one bunch of fellows gather in a circle and study the ground. Before astro-turf I used to think they were looking for bugs, but now I don't know what they're looking for. Anyway, they suddenly trot over to where the other team is waiting, and apparently they tell them to look too, because soon they're all bending over and staring. Before they find whatever they're looking for, some fellow—the same one I asked my husband about—runs away from these two groups. At the same time the others are fighting, and all over a deformed-looking ball.

You would think, as popular as football is, they'd have a round ball, and more than one so the fellows would quit acting so ugly over it.

They are very rude, snatching, hitting, and grabbing each other around the legs. When the strongest one gets it he runs off in one direction, then in another, apparently confused as to what to do with it. I think they have a vision problem because of those face protectors. They are forever running into one another!

The announcers aren't very good at explaining either.

"I think that's disgraceful," I shouted, during the game. "If he hadn't been drunk, he'd probably play better."

"Drunk?" For once I had my husband's attention. "Who?"

"Howard just said that fellow was tight."

He shook his head. "He was talking about the tight *end*. See that fellow right over there by the wide receiver?"

"They all look about the same size to me."

My husband shut me out again—just when I thought I would learn something. However, one thing I have learned. When the clock says there is five minutes left to play, that means they'll be playing at least another twenty or thirty minutes.

No one can comprehend what goes on under the sun. (Eccl. 8:17)

Before I invited Christ to take charge, I was as confused over the game of life as I am about football. Now, because of His "coaching" I know who I am and where I'm going and how I am going to get there.

We know ... the Son of God has come and has given us understanding. (1 John 5:20)

152

Columbus Day

In high school, American History was probably my worst subject, next to World History or Geometry. I could not remember dates. To this day, even if my life depended upon it, I could not tell you when Daniel Boone made the Louisiana Purchase. And I have no idea when they first sailed Old Ironsides through the Erie Canal. I'm not even sure when Abraham Lincoln married Barbara Fritchie. One date I am certain about, however, is that Columbus discovered America in 1492. I don't know why that date is so indelibly inscribed on my brain. I've often wondered what the teacher said to make 1492 stand out when all other dates are hopelessly lost in my gray matter. When I help the kids and quiz them on American History dates, it's as though I never heard any of them before. Yet, the other night, watching a quiz show they asked when Columbus discovered America, and I piped right up: "1492!" The family was amazed, and I let them be impressed. I hate for them to find out that is the only date I know.

Even in more recent history I haven't the foggiest idea about dates. I ought to know when the Hindenburg sank after running into an iceberg, but I don't. I don't even know when Glen Campbell landed on the moon. But I know Columbus discovered America in 1492.

I don't suppose it is really going to hurt that I can't remember any of these dates—but I wish I could remember from one year to the next that the banks are closed on Columbus Day.

Our days on earth are like a shadow. (1 Chron. 29:15)

I am not the only one who can't remember historical dates, and it points up an important fact. No matter how great a person was, or what he accomplished, the only date that matters in the light of eternity is the date he accepted Christ as Savior.

The LORD reigns forever. (Ps. 9:7)

Fall Housecleaning

"Are you moving?" I called to my neighbor two doors down as I watched her husband bring out an overstuffed chair and place it beside the couch on the driveway.

"No—just doing fall cleaning!" she called back.

I walked down the sidewalk as she came toward me.

"Are you getting new carpeting?" I asked.

"No, no. My husband is going to shampoo the old one."

"You mean you have to move everything outside to shampoo?"

"Sure. That's how professionals do it."

"I know, but, my—all that work. Nobody can see under the furniture."

She looked at me as though I had just sworn at her.

"I *always* move the furniture, even to vacuum," she sniffed.

"You do?" I marveled.

"Of course! Don't you?"

"Oh! Well, yes—uh—at least when I change the furniture around."

She looked down at me. "I move everything, every week, and vacuum thoroughly. That way you don't get moths." She paused. "Or any other bugs."

Back in my house I began to itch. How long had it been since I vacuumed under the furniture? I couldn't remember doing any spring cleaning.

In our bedroom, half afraid, I peered under the bed. The gold shag carpeting seemed much thicker there.

"Probably because it doesn't get any wear," I mumbled, but in my heart I knew that extra inch was pure fuzz.

I sank down on the unmade bed and sighed. Rats. I had planned to look through the new Sears catalog this morning, and drink coffee and eat a piece of roll I had hidden. But I knew I couldn't enjoy it, not knowing what was lurking in all that fuzz. I leaped off the bed.

"To battle!" I cried, and with a mighty yank I pulled the covers off the bed, sending magazines and cats flying into the air.

"You changed the bedroom around," my husband said that night as he maneuvered around the dresser.

I looked down at him, trying to imitate my neighbor.

"You know I always like to move everything when I vacuum! That's why we don't have any moths."

She [a wife of noble character] watches over the affairs of her household and does not eat the bread of idleness. (Prov. 31:27)

I feel guilty enough for allowing fuzz-buildup. But I feel even worse that my neighbor sees me go off to church every Sunday, and then finds out I don't vacuum under the furniture. And worst of all is to remember that *God* sees everything!

The eyes of the LORD are everywhere. (Prov. 15:3)

156

The Coffin

Next Halloween I think I'll refuse to be in charge of the Young People's party. It was too unnerving, even though at first it seemed like fun and a challenge.

"Everything has to be really scary," Ron told me, "or the kids will be bored."

"Scary, huh?" I smirked. "I'll make you kids a haunted house you'll never forget!"

"Hee, hee!" I cackled, when I was by myself. "So they want to be scared!"

I stuffed one leg of pantyhose with cotton, put a high heel shoe on it, put the leg in a suitcase and dabbed catsup at the top. That horrible sight would have a flashlight shinning on it in one of the dark corridors I planned to make with blankets, clothespins, and line.

"No haunted house is complete without a hanging!" I shrieked.

I stuffed a pair of coveralls with newspapers. Then I attached shoes, a stocking head, and a rope. The shadow he cast swinging from a beam scared even me.

In an iron skillet I put a rubber mask in the center, dumped catsup all around it and whispered to myself, "Fried face, anyone?"

The pièce de résistance was the *coffin,* made from a refrigerator box. I set the box on its side, cut the top so that it would open casket style, and covered the outside with black material. I filled the coffin with more wadded-up newspapers, then covered the inside with a sheet. The body was furnished by my husband—his old clothes stuffed with newspapers, and a rubber mask for the head.

I put the rest of the things in the wagon and started for church. I was within two blocks of the church when I had to stop for a red light. I glanced in the rear view mirror and there was a police car. The two officers were straining to see inside my car. My heart began to pound. Surely they wouldn't think it was a real body, would they?

They had a brief conference, and then they pulled along my right side. They stared at the coffin, then at me. I pretended not to notice and when the light changed I turned left. They did too, even though they were in the wrong lane. They followed me to the church parking lot. By this time my heart was banging against my rib cage. I turned in, and held my breath. Praises! They went on by.

At home that night, after the party, Ron said, "That was a pretty good haunted house, Mother. Not scary, but fun."

Not scary? I couldn't believe it. It scared the living daylights out of me. Yes sir—some braver person can take charge next Halloween.

I will ransom them from the power of the grave. (Hos. 13:14)

We don't have to fear death—not even at Halloween! Death is frightening for those who don't know Jesus, but for Christians it is the means for us to be with the Lord.

Where, O death, is your victory? (1 Cor. 15:55)

Whistle Bait

Two beautiful young women have moved in across the street. One day, while they were working outside, I decided to welcome them and invite them to church, so I chose a plant to give them and crossed the street.

I found out they are even more beautiful at close range than from across the street. They both have long, dark hair, beautiful figures, which they show off in their tight, tight jeans. It made me sick to look at them, they're so gorgeous, but I couldn't quit staring.

While we were standing on the lawn talking, some fellows went by in a Corvette. They slammed on their brakes, blew the horn, and whistled. In fact, every time the girls step outside, somebody toots his horn or whistles.

It's been a long time since any fellow whistled or tooted his horn at me. In fact, this morning I felt as if I belonged in Leisure World when the box boy at the store said, "Can you manage one bag by yourself, ma'am?"

Ma'am? Ma'am indeed! Grrrr!

Maybe my eyebrows are the reason men don't whistle. They're thick and black, and I'm too cowardly to pluck them to a thin line the way the girls across the street do. But I know having skinny eyebrows alone won't help.

I can't zip up my old blue jeans, much less get that Jordache Look. I'm not really fat, because I can still use a size twelve pattern, if I allow for half an inch. But I sure don't look like the new neighbors.

Maybe my hair is another reason fellows don't whistle any more. It's short and straight, and I know fellows love long hair. But every time I vow I'm going to let it grow long, and it gets to the shaggy stage, people start saying things like, "Aren't you feeling well?" or "I didn't know you'd been sick."

In K-Mart the other day I decided to try on a long, dark wig to see if I should let my hair grow again. I couldn't believe the transformation—instant witch. Long hair is out, for me.

Probably what I need to make the fellows notice is a whole new wardrobe. The girls across the street have so many beautiful clothes. I've already seen them in more outfits in a week than I've owned since I got married.

I feel grumpy and I don't know why. Should it bother me so much that fellows don't whistle any more?

No!

But—boo, hoo—it does.

Turn my eyes away from worthless things; renew my life according to your word. (Ps. 119:37)

I've got my eyes on *self* again—I even forgot to invite the girls to church. (Probably my subconscious, hoping they wouldn't accept.) *Lord!* I need Your help. I'm acting as ugly as I feel—*covetous.*

Put off your old self . . . and put on the new self, created to be like God. (Eph. 4:22–24)

What Can You Say When They Say, "You Said"?

I think I am going to the stationery store and buy some contracts, agreements, promissory notes, memo pads, and a big sign that reads: *"Don't say it—write it."* I've had it with my friends, mother, and husband telling me I said something I know I did not say—or worse, denying *they* said something I *know* they said.

When I went to mother's, the minute I walked in she said, "Did you bring the stamps?"

"What stamps?"

"Honey—" in her exasperated voice. "I gave you two dollars and you said you'd buy me some stamps."

I looked at the little lady before me. Yes, this was my mother, but I had no recollection of her giving me any money. But, you don't call your mother a liar, so I bought the stamps. Next time I'll make her fill out a purchase order.

And my husband is always claiming or denying he said something—"I *did* tell you Vera called," or "You *did not* tell me the gas tank was empty." Awhile back in a restaurant I distinctly remember his very words: "One of my favorite salads is spinach and mushrooms."

So, always eager to please, I made a big spinach and mushroom salad the next night.

He carefully picked out the mushrooms.

"What are you *doing?*" I howled.

161

"Can't stand mushrooms," he said.

"But you *said*—" I was near tears.

"Not me. You've got me mixed up with somebody else."

And my best friend—we were to meet for lunch by the escalators on the first level of the mall. I finally found her on the second level—and she was mad at *me*.

"You told me *second* level," she declared.

We didn't really quarrel, but it sort of ruined our lunch. That's why I'm not going to talk to anyone in the future without a paper and pen. In fact—I *had* written down our lunch date—here it is! Ah, hah! "Meet Louise. Noon . . ." Hmm . . . "Second level."

Wonder if there are any of those signs at the store that say, "Be Patient—God Isn't Finished With Me"?

Do not think of yourself more highly than you ought, but rather think of yourself with sober judgment. (Rom. 12:3)

It's amazing how positive I can be that I'm right, only to learn I was mistaken.

Do not entertain an accusation . . . unless it is brought by two or three witnesses. (1 Tim. 5:19)

Delayed Disease

Our family is a bunch of hypochondriacs. No matter what symptoms I have, it isn't long until either my husband or the kids have the same thing, only worse. Many, many times when the aches and sneezes have grabbed me, I've promised myself a day in bed. But before I can get the covers back, somebody else in the family doubles over in pain, sneezes three times, and clutches his or her throat. Naturally my petty illness has to be postponed while I administer first aid, aspirin, and Vicks.

This doesn't happen just with colds. If I remark, for instance, that my eyes hurt and I better get my eyes examined, the whole family suddenly begins to Magoo around and look for the Murine.

The last time my back was out of whack I called the chiropractor. I told the receptionist she might as well make two appointments, because somebody in the family would need it. Sure enough, before my back improved, my husband began to walk around with his shoulder hunched up because *his* back hurt. Instead of getting the attention I thought I deserved, I found myself looking for electrical outlets. I was plugging in the heating pad wherever His Miserable Self decided to sit down.

Two weeks ago an aggravating cough attacked me. It's irritating to cough all the time, but I can cope with my own cough. What's hard is listening to everyone else. Our home sounds like the dog pound at feeding time.

For the family's good I think I'll teach them all a lesson (and get the attention I deserve). Tomorrow, I think I'll have a toothache.

We do not lose heart. Though outwardly we are wasting away. (2 Cor. 4:16)

As a wife and mother it's my job—and my desire—to pamper everyone else, even when I yearn to be pampered myself. But one of these days, when I am with the *Lord,* He will baby *me,* He will pamper me—even wipe every tear from my eyes!

We wait for the blessed hope. (Titus 2:13)

November

Sample Ballot

"Who are you voting for in the gubernatorial election?" my neighbor asked.

"I thought we were voting for governor," I answered.

"We are! Who are you voting for?"

"I'll probably vote for whoever my husband chooses."

"What?" she scoffed. "Don't tell me you're one of those. In the thirteen years I've been married I've almost never voted the same as my husband."

"Then your votes just cancel each other."

"So? Aren't you a person? Don't you have a mind?"

After she went home I picked up the sample ballot.

"Maybe I should study this thing," I murmured to myself. "After all, I am a person. I have a mind."

I read the first page aloud:

"Voting instructions, instrucciones para votar . . ."

Hmm. Wonder if ballots in Mexico are also printed in English? . . . My word, what a lot of candidates for governor. I thought there would only be two. Let's see—

"Charles Steven, Governor; Walter Toms, Lieutenant Governor, Republican . . ."

I don't like the name of that first candidate—too confusing. I would probably call him Steven Charles. And Walter Toms—I'd get that name turned around for sure. Anyway, I don't much care for the name 'Walter,' ever since I saw a dog on TV named Walter. I don't believe I'll vote for those two.

"James Clark and Clement Davidson, Democrats . . ."

Wonder if by any chance James Clark is related to my uncle Ed Clark? Of course Uncle Ed was a staunch Republican, so they probably aren't related. Or maybe they are, and this James Clark is wishy-washy and can't decide what party he is for. We surely don't need indecisive people in government. And Clement sounds like cement. Wonder if he has a hard head? Hee, hee. Well—I don't think either of these would be a good gubernate, or whatever she said.

"Deanna Morris, Jack Commoner, Independent . . ."

Deanna! Just think! A girl—I mean, a woman, running for governor in our state! All right! That's who I'll vote for. But wait a moment—Jack Commoner? A commoner for lieutenant governor? Doesn't sound right. Now I don't know what to do. This studying is hard! And look at all these other things—school bonds, flood control, busing, anti-pollution—the way they're worded I don't know if I'm for them or against them. Rats. This is no fun. I won't let my neighbor know, but I think I'll just copy my husband's ballot.

Submit yourselves for the Lord's sake to every authority instituted among men. (1 Peter 2:13)

There is plenty of evidence in the Bible that the *Lord* wants me to be a good citizen so I won't bring shame on the name of Christ—even if it means studying a boring ballot so I will vote right.

You are the salt of the earth. (Matt. 5:13)

Thanksgiving with Mr. D

"What are you doing for Thanksgiving?" Aunt Barbara asked.

"Nothing special," I answered hopefully. Aunt Barbara is probably the best cook in our family and has a big house. "Why?"

"Just wondered what you'd be doing. We didn't want you to feel left out—"

"Ye-e-ss?"

"—because we've decided to invite four little old ladies at the church this year instead of the family."

"Oh." I sighed. "How nice."

Rats. I thought she was going to invite us to dinner.

But what a thoughtful idea! I should do something like that, too. In fact, one Thanksgiving several years ago I did invite a lonely old gentleman from the church to dinner.

"Thank you so much!" old Mr. Deevoe said, with teeth clacking. He evidently had never heard of denture adhesives, because his teeth were always loose, and sometimes they stayed shut, even though his mouth was open. This gave him a startling appearance, sort of like a rabid dog.

"Haven't had a real home-cooked Thanksgiving meal since my wife went to be with the Lord," he clacked.

We all worked hard to give Mr. D a happy Thanksgiving. My husband drove across town to pick him up. Meanwhile Ron prettied up the yard and Joan and I labored over the meal. We had the whole traditional menu—turkey, dressing, sweet potatoes, mashed potatoes, giblet gravy, cranberries, green beans with cheese sauce, homemade rolls (frozen Bridgeford), fruit salad, green salad, pumpkin and mince pies with whipped cream.

But dinner was a disaster. He couldn't eat sweet potatoes because of an allergy; mashed potatoes and dressing were out because of the seasonings; he couldn't chew the green salad, and "I can't stand green beans, much less with cheese on 'em." However, he did eat a lot of turkey, hot bread, minced pie and whipped cream—which made him sick.

When he began feeling better later he told us. "It was worth bein' sick, not to be alone on Thanksgiving."

He died just before Christmas that year. I don't know if my dinner had anything to do with it or not, but I am glad we included old Mr. D on that Thanksgiving Day. Wonder if old George down the street has any plans for Thanksgiving?

Offer hospitality to one another without grumbling. (1 Peter 4:9)

As I get older I have to admit I am less hospitable, and more selfish with my time. Shame, shame on me! Jesus, my Example, is continually inviting people to His Marriage Supper. As I look at Him, how can I refuse to be hospitable?

Go ... invite to the banquet anyone you find. (Matt. 22:9)

Cyclops

Just the sight of our bathroom scale weighs me down. Every morning it crouches there, with its wicked Cyclops eye staring at me until I am compelled to step on it. Morning by morning it angers, discourages, or humiliates me.

If only it would sometimes have a positive message. At best it's grudgingly the same. At least two mornings a week its evil eye shows a gain. In order to stay approximately the same weight I have to literally starve a couple of days a week.

Thanksgiving Day I felt guilty about everything I ate, and Friday morning, when Cyclops beckoned to me, I dreaded to find out the bad news. At last I eased up to him, carefully put first one foot, then the other on his back, then apprehensively looked him in the eye.

What? *Oh joy!* I hadn't gained! *I hadn't gained!* I felt like Snoopy as I twirled around on one foot. I was so happy I ate a cold sweet potato. At lunch I ate turkey, pecan pie, and then a small piece of pumpkin pie—with Cool Whip. In the afternoon, during Christmas shopping, I treated myself to a sack of popcorn. That night, I ate a potato chip— and you know nobody can eat just one.

So it went through the weekend—popcorn, nuts, snacks—even before breakfast, my stomach looked as though I was with child. I dragged myself to the bathroom for the daily confrontation.

Rats! I knew old tattlescale would give a bad report! With a vindictive whirr he announced a gain of *four* pounds.

So I have to fast the rest of the week. I've got to lose a lot of weight before Christmas. We'll have all that yummy, traditional food—I can hardly wait.

I wonder—if I gave a check to World Vision—could I get off Cyclops' back?

Now if I do what I do not want to do, it is no longer I who do it, but it is sin living in me that does it. (Rom. 7:20)

When I let Joanie drive, I get out of the driver's seat and hand her the keys. I commit myself and the car to her control. Lord Jesus, here are the keys to my appetite. Take control—please!

The mind controlled by the Spirit is life and peace. (Rom. 8:6)

Spec-ulation

Do people ever get used to wearing glasses? I've been trying for quite a while, but I can't make myself keep them on long enough to get used to them. One reason is because when I got my first pair, everything far away looked blurry, so I would take them off. But without them, everything up close was blurry, so I would put them on. I got in the habit of taking them off, putting them on, taking them off—and losing them.

"Bifocals would fix that," my friend Mary said.

I got a pair, but then, at a distance everything looked tiny and curved, and people up close had a line through their stomach and very short legs. The glasses also affected my equilibrium. One of my neighbors thought I was on drugs because when I walk with my glasses on I lift my feet like a cat on a wet sidewalk.

"You'll be a lot better off," Mary said, "if you'll make yourself wear them and get used to it."

"Why don't you try contacts?" my nephew urged. He had just bought a pair himself. "They're great!"

I didn't tell him, but I already have tried them. When my Cucamonga girl friend got hers I foolishly asked, "What do they feel like?"

"Not bad," she said, blinking rapidly. "Sort of like an eyelash."

"How awful!"

"It's not really that bad," she assured me. "Let me show you."

She pushed me into a chair, blinked a contact into her hand, rinsed it, and popped it in on my pupil. It felt as though she had tossed hot sand in my eye.

"Get it out! Get it out!" I squalled.

"Be calm!" she screamed, shaking her hands. "Blink! It'll pop right out!"

I did, but it didn't. Finally, she got a hammerlock on me and got her lens back.

Mary is right, I know, and I have been making myself wear the glasses more, to get used to them. In fact, I guess I am getting more comfortable with them—I wore them to bed last night.

No one knows about that day or hour, not even the angels in heaven, nor the Son, but only the Father. (Matt. 24:36)

I'm glad I'm getting more used to my glasses—but it reminds me of something the pastor said in a sermon:

"Don't get too used to your life, too comfortable. Don't get your roots in too deep. Watch, and be ready to go."

The day of the Lord will come like a thief in the night. (1 Thess. 5:2)

Helps

"Helpful Hints" columns always get my attention. How to take off white rings from varnished surfaces; how to remove candle wax from your mother's best lace cloth; how to get baby oil out of your sister's carpet—all those hints are so great. I have probably cut out and saved a hundred columns. Unfortunately, I can never find them when I need them. But I still read them, and recently, I have thought maybe I could write one.

For example, I wonder how many people know that an easy way to remove cat or dog hair from your clothes is simply to wet the palms of your hands with ordinary tap water, then run your hands all over your clothes? The hair balls up on your hands and makes a revolting mess, but it sure takes it off your clothes.

Another useful thing I'm sure not many people know is that white paint spots on black slacks can be covered nicely with a black marker pen. Also, I covered a spaghetti sauce spot on the lapel of my white blazer with white Liquid Paper! Ingenious?

If you want to press the side seam of a pant leg, or a sleeve and don't own a sleeveboard, just slip a book inside and press! (Be sure it's a book you don't want to read again, as the steam tends to make the pages stick together.)

If you're in a hurry and don't want to set up the ironing

board, press your clothes on the bed. It's best to throw back the electric blanket—I have a suspicion that may be the reason my side of the blanket won't heat.

Have you put on a little weight and have difficulty zipping up your jeans? Lie down on your back and you will be amazed how your stomach seems to fall into a hole. Then you can zip right up.

Aren't these suggestions helpful?

That's enough material right there for my first column! I wonder what I should call it?

And in the church God has appointed ... those able to help others. (1 Cor. 12:28)

The problem I have in helping others is that I always want to do it my way, and the person I'm trying to help, ends up helping me. *Help me,* Lord Jesus, not to be bossy, but to be humble enough to take orders.

You help us by your prayers. (2 Cor. 1:11)

Ugly Is in the Eye
of the Beholder

The other day I decided I despised every piece of clothing I own. There wasn't one thing in that closet I really liked. I yanked down a pair of red slacks that make me look like a barrel on stilts and threw them on the floor. In quick jerks, before I could change my mind, I tossed in a pair of baggy black pants, a faded muumuu, and three blouses that either had buttons off or made me look flat chested. I also threw a couple of long, double-knit dresses on the pile.

"Nobody wears these things anymore," I muttered. "In fact, nobody would wear anything I own!"

I jammed all the clothes I had thrown on the floor into a grocery sack and marched out to the car.

"Someday," I promised myself, "I'll throw away all my clothes and buy some gorgeous things that make me look like—" I glanced across the street "—those new neighbors!"

The phone was ringing when I came back in the house.

"I'm cleaning out closets," one of the beauties said. "Does your church have a program for collecting old clothes?"

I licked my lips with anticipation.

"I'll be right over!"

At home I dumped her sack of clothes out on the bed and feverishly began to try them on.

"What beautiful blouses she's throwing away!" I whispered as I turned this way and that to see how I looked. "And look at these black slacks!" In a moment I put them on, and although I had to struggle with the zipper I finally got them fastened. Beautiful! "Oh, oh! Look at these long dresses—how gorgeous!"

I was glad I had empty hangers from my old clothes. Within seconds everything was hanging up.

Later in the day she thanked me for helping her get rid of her old clothes.

"Everything I have looks so old and ugly," her beautiful lips pouted. "I just hate my clothes. Someday, I promise you, I'm going to throw away everything and buy all new!"

Therefore I tell you, do not worry about your life, what you will eat or drink; or about your body, what you will wear. Is not life more important than food, and the body more important than clothes? (Matt. 6:25)

Every time I get my eye on "I" I get crabby, but when I focus on *Him,* I am happy. Why can't I remember that it isn't all-important to be *in style?* The only all-important thing is to be *in Christ.*

He is kind to the ungrateful. (Luke 6:35) Thank You, Lord!

An X on Ten

The thought of having to learn the metric system is frightening. I've never been able to memorize my social security number or license plate. I don't think I can handle the switch to an entirely new system of measurement.

We got a folder in the mail called "Conversion Factors with Metric," and it's supposed to be an instant course in the system. But I can't understand the first page.

Words like kilogram, liter, millimeter—I feel as if I'm on another planet. I never was good in math; the only reason I didn't fail in geometry is because the teacher couldn't face having me another semester. My husband is fantastic with figures, but there is a mathematical piece missing from my brain. I was a grown woman before I memorized 5,280 feet make a mile. How can I ever remember it in meters? How can I even if I can find out how many meters there are in a mile? I'll never be able to learn it! What if someone speaks to me in metric-ese? I won't know my celsius from my kilogram.

They say we will even have recipes in metric. I shudder to think what the outcome will be, from my translation. And just when I was beginning to feel at ease pumping my own gas, I drove into a station with brand-new pumps. When the meter began to click off *liters* I spilled gas all over the back tire. I never did know how many gallons I got. All I know is it cost me fifteen dollars American. I hate it! But I have to learn it. Back to the folder!

Hey! One good thing—I'll weigh less in kilograms than pounds. That's encouraging. Possibly, there might be some virtue to a system based on ten. I will at least try to learn it. It might be ten times easier than I think.

[*The Lord said,*] *"My grace is sufficient for you, for my power is made perfect in weakness." (2 Cor. 12:9)*

A new situation makes me anxious, but the Lord always helps me get through—pregnancies, deaths, moving—He never fails.

Do not let your hearts be troubled. Trust in God; trust also in me. (John 14:1)

December

Visions of Sugar—
Plumb Gone

Aunt Barbara is now the healthiest member of our family. She's been studying nutrition, and putting into practice what she has learned. Her eyes are bright, her skin glows, and she exhorts a lot.

"You *must* quit eating sugars!" Her brown eyes were wide with alarm. "Sugar causes headaches, pains, colds—and I ought to know—it's poison! You might as well be eating strychnine!"

"Maybe you're right," I answered uncomfortably. "But this is a dumb time to give up sugar. It wouldn't be the Christmas season without fudge, cake, pie, brownies, cookies, candy—" My mouth was watering.

"Oh, tush. There are lots of good things to eat," she said and gave me a sugar-free cookbook. "Look—desserts made with pineapple, bananas, apples—*And,*" she eyed me triumphantly, "these won't cause tooth decay."

Tooth decay. I had to admit that was a terrible result of sugar. But a Christmas without traditional goodies?
Depressing!

After she went home, instead of looking at the cookbook, I picked up the Bible. Maybe I could find a verse or two that supported eating sugar. The Bible fell open at Luke:

"And she brought forth her firstborn Son, and wrapped Him in swaddling clothes, and laid Him in a manger—"

I began to think about Jesus. First He was the Baby, then the Boy preaching in the temple, and finally, the Man.

"When Jesus was a man," I wondered, "what kind of foods did He eat? Did He like sweets? Did He ever have a toothache?"

"Such sacrilege!" my goody-self said.

"I don't think it's sacrilege. He was a man, so wouldn't He have to suffer like the rest of us?"

"But remember, He was also God, so maybe He was immune to earthly pain."

"Yes, but the Bible says He *suffered* when He hung on the cross. Think how His joints ached as He hung there, the excruciating pain in his hands and feet, how his back hurt as He was crucified for *my* sins!" I couldn't stand to think about it.

Okay, Aunt Barbara—I'll try some of these recipes. If Jesus was willing to take on all human suffering, including toothaches and crucifixion, just so my sins could be forgiven, just so I could be saved, the least I can do is take care of this body.

For we do not have a high priest who is unable to sympathize with our weaknesses, but we have one who has been tempted in every way, just as we are. (Heb. 4:15)

What a disappointment I must be to the *Lord*. He gave up heaven to be crucified for me—and I abuse the body He died for. Lord, help me to change.

And she gave birth to her firstborn, a son (Luke 2:7)

Fourteen Days

I'm getting panicky! Only fourteen days until Christmas, and I've barely started my tasks! Gifts to buy, cards to write, baking to do! Oh, why do I do this every year? In September, when the kids went back to school, my guardian angel warned, "Now is the time to get started on Christmas."

"You are so right," I agreed. "I'll start knitting some dish cloths, and finish painting that nativity set I started, and buy all the presents, and get them wrapped and—"

But Satan drawled, "You have three whole months—what's the hurry?"

In October, every time I went shopping I thought, I *ought to buy something.* But I kept putting it off—I didn't know sizes, or favorite colors, or what they already had. In November I still hadn't bought a gift.

On Thanksgiving some of the neighbors were talking about the Christmas gifts they had bought. I smiled as though I had some secrets put away also, but the only secret I had was that I was not ready for Christmas.

How can some people be so well organized? We've already received lots of Christmas cards, but mine aren't even addressed.

Fourteen days! What am I going to do? If only I could win a trip to Hawaii and be gone for the holidays—

"Listen, Mab," Satan murmured, "you only have twelve presents to buy, right?"

"True."

"Very well. If you only buy two a day, that would take six of your fourteen days. It won't take you over one day to do your Christmas cards—and you can do a lot of baking in one day; clean your house in one day, and wrap presents one day. Ten days will do it all, and you will have four glorious days to enjoy Christmas—"

Fourteen days! Why was I so panicky? That's a *lot* of time.

Go to the ant, you sluggard; consider its ways and be wise! . . . it stores its provisions in summer and gathers its food at harvest. (Prov. 6:6, 8)

Every year Satan whispers his lie, "There is plenty of time." In this way he robs me of some of the joy of Christmas. How much more tragic is this lie for those who have not yet received the Christ of Christmas!

Today, if you hear his voice, do not harden your hearts. (Heb. 3:15)

Post Office

Have you ever noticed how quiet it is in the post office? People drive up, laughing and talking, but the minute they are inside, within those pale green walls a pall envelopes them and they become morose and silent.

The only place quieter than the post office is another post office. The folks in our church on Sunday morning make more noise than people buying stamps.

I was in line yesterday for seventeen minutes, and during that time the only voice I heard was the postal clerk. She made occasional tomb-like comments, such as:

"You can't send it like that."

"This weighs too much."

"This can't be insured."

Each time, the customers looked stricken, but they didn't argue. Like zombies, they turned and walked away silently.

What happens to us in the post office? If we were in line at a football game we would be wisecracking, laughing, talking. Even people in line at the supermarket talk to each other. But at the PO we stand like statues, staring ahead in silence. Is it because we are surrounded by pictures of most-wanted criminals? Is it because we're trying to decide if the letters in our hands are worth almost ten times more postage than they were not so many years ago? Or are we stunned because the flag on the fifteen-cent stamp has eight red stripes? Whatever it is, the post office is depressing.

I wish I had the nerve to dress up in some ridiculous outfit, and like one of those singing telegram people, burst into the quiet chamber, maybe at noon when it is full of silent spooks, and start singing as loud as I can:

> O-o say can you see,
>   a-ny-one filled with glee?
> What'-s so sad a-bout stamps,
>   that we all stand here griev-ing?
> Just be-cause one quick lick
>   makes us all feel quite sick
> Is no rea-son to cry!
>   U-ni-ted Par-cel's near-by.
> O-o say does you-r P O
>   sti-l ge-t you down?
> There is just one thing to do—
>   be a clown, be a clown!

Shout with joy to God, all the earth! Sing to the glory of his name; offer Him glory and praise! (Ps. 66:1)

Oil can't gush out of the top of a well if there isn't any oil down in the ground; joy won't bubble up on the outside of a person if there isn't any joy on the inside. O thank You, Lord, for putting Your joy in me!

The joy of the LORD is your strength. (Neh. 8:10)

Let Us Spray

The consumer advocate on TV pointed a finger at me.

"If you, the purchaser, will refuse to accept faulty merchandise, then production standards will have to come up."

His brown eyes sparked with anger.

"What should *you* do when you find you have purchased a product which weighs less than the label states, or will not function as promised?"

He paused for dramatic effect, then stared out at me. "You take it back and get a refund or a replacement!"

"I'm going to take back that can of hairspray I got today," I said to my husband.

"What's wrong with it?"

"It won't spray. It oozes."

"Let's see it."

I brought the can to him and he pushed the head from every angle, took it off and blew in it and tried again.

"You're right. It doesn't work. Take it back."

At the supermarket I showed the can to a checker.

"I either want to exchange it, or get my money back," I declared.

"I'll call the manager," she said. She summoned him over the loudspeaker, then stood there, while the people in line began to frown at me. Pretty soon a huge, angry-looking man charged up to the counter. The checker stated the problem to the manager.

"How much was it?" he growled. "Did you take off the price?" He turned it around in his beefy hand. "Got your receipt?"

"No—but I give you my word, I bought it here."

"Crumb," he grumbled. "Have to look it up." He banged the can down on the counter and began to thumb through a sheaf of papers. The checker picked up the can.

"Whadja say was wrong with it?" she asked, but before I could answer she had sprayed both of us. "Seems to work okay now." She grinned at me.

I tried it. It worked perfectly. I smiled sheepishly, tucked the can in my purse, and tiptoed away from the manager.

The next night the TV fellow was still scolding: "As I pointed out last night—"

"Did you take back that hairspray?" my husband asked.

I thought for a moment. Well—I *had* taken it back—I lifted my chin.

"Certainly. We consumers have to set the standards."

Have nothing to do with the fruitless deeds of darkness, but rather expose them. (Eph. 5:11)

Lots of times it is easier for me to "let it go" than to speak up for what is right. I'm really pretty cowardly and hate to make waves—but the Lord has given me the inner strength to speak up for myself, and also, to speak out for *Him*.

Put on the full armor of God, so that when ... evil comes, you may be able to stand your ground. (Eph. 6:13)

One Is Not Enough

Isn't it amazing that everybody, both men and women, is wearing gold today? They say women can tell if it's really gold, but I can't. I do wonder sometimes—especially when I see beauties with a four- or five-chain necklace, each chain decorated with gold charms that cost twenty dollars and up—if they are real gold. How can they afford it?

One day I asked a saleswoman with a bib of chains if all of it was real gold. She looked as upset as if I had asked her if she used Dial.

"*I* wouldn't *wear* anything that wasn't genuine!" she said in a huff.

Personally, I like my little Monet gold-color chain my sis gave me. It sparkles even more than my one very, very, *very* thin 14K chain the folks at the office gave me when I quit.

Is that how women can tell if it's genuine—the more glitter the less gold?

All of it is beautiful and I would love to have more. However, I have quite a bit of trouble with the few status symbols I own now. Besides the Monet chain, and the 14K gold "hair," I also have a 10K bracelet (very thin) that Joanie gave me and a pair of gold loop earrings my husband bought.

I wear all of it all the time. You can't be too careful with your valuables, you know. But they do bother me. My

191

chains never lay quietly on my sweater nor look elegant like other ladies' chains. Mine tangle among themselves, and their fasteners hang down in front.

And they also bother me when I'm in bed. Several times a night I awake with my loops folded back the wrong way. This hurts my ears, and the chains twist so tightly around my neck they almost choke me.

"Why do you wear that junk all the time?" my husband asked. "Shouldn't you at least take it off when you go to bed?"

He shook his head with disgust. "Every time you turn over you sound like a wind chime."

"Yes, but what if the house got on fire, and I had to jump up and run out? I would have to leave my valuables behind!" I answered sternly.

"Besides, what if someone came to see me in the morning. I wouldn't want to be seen without my *gold*."

For you know that it was not with perishable things such as silver or gold that you were redeemed from the empty way of life . . . but with the precious blood of Christ. (1 Peter 1:18–19)

When I read what the Bible says about gold, I wonder if I should give away my jewelry? And yet, the trinkets were given to me as gifts of love. Maybe, instead of wanting *more,* I should be *willing* to give it all away, if God asks me to.

How much better to get wisdom than gold. (Prov. 16:16)

The Terrible Tardies

My family and friends know I'm usually a few minutes late wherever I go. I'm ashamed of this habit, and I've made many resolutions and promises to change. I straighten up for a while, but gradually I slip back into the terrible tardies.

My husband, however, is super speedy. He's never late. What's worse, he's always early.

There is one good result of this situation. When we go places together, while we may not be one minute early, at least we're never late.

I don't know how he manages to put up with this problem, but he never nags. He might come to the bedroom door and look at his watch, or offer to take out my curlers, or start turning out the lights, but he never says, "Hurry up!"

Recently, though, he has started collecting clocks. He says it's a hobby, but I have my suspicions.

Who else has two clocks in the living room, two in the kitchen, two in the bedroom, and one in the den? I took the initiative and got one for the bathroom. I knew it wouldn't be long before he put one there too.

With all these clocks, you'd think I would now be on time, right? Not so! And there are two reasons:

First, one clock seldom agrees with another. Naturally, I go by the one that gives me the most time. When I told my husband that, he synchronized them. But that didn't solve the problem, because of reason number two.

You see, there are always stacks of things in front of the clocks. In the den for example, the stapler and postage scale are in front of the clock. In the bedroom, a box of tissues and the Bible often hide that timepiece. And on the dresser a can of hair spray, a perfume bottle, and some books often block the view to that clock. In the bathroom somebody put my deodorant right in front of the clock.

I think I'm destined to be late. Even my watch slips evasively around my wrist so I can't see the face.

Do you think people mind if I'm a bit tardy? I hope that old adage is true: better late than never.

There is a time for everything, and a season for every activity under heaven. (Eccl. 3:1)

I've asked the Lord to tell me why I can't seem to get ready on time. The answer is: I love myself more than others! What a disheartening discovery. But it's true. If I really love others, I won't keep them waiting.

In everything, do to others what you would have them do to you. (Matt. 7:12)

Spray by Braille

Wouldn't it be wonderful if manufacturers would make labels you could feel as well as read? I'm sure I wouldn't have had all the extra messes to clean up this week if I could have *felt* the labels on the spray cans I used.

We were expecting company from Colorado and I was hurrying to get things reasonably clean before they came. I grabbed a can from under the sink and sprayed the oven. But it didn't look like oven cleaner. It looked like snow.

I squinted and read the label. It *was* snow. Artificial snow.

I groaned, grabbed another can and sprayed the oven again. The snow began to melt and turn to grease. I squinted again. *Pam!*

"Idiot!" I screamed. The cat squalled and raced down the hall, tail flying.

On the third try I got the right can, but it took a long time to get the oven clean.

Then I decided to tackle the windows. I sprayed the window over the sink, but when I started to polish it, I learned that *Raid* does not do a very sparkly job on windows.

At last the house looked pretty nice, so I showered and got dressed up. I took a lot of trouble curling my hair, then sprayed it thoroughly with—*air freshener!* I smelled more piney that night than the Christmas tree.

None of these things would have happened if I could have felt the labels. I don't know just how the manufacturers could do this—maybe they could have, for example, spray cleaners with a little square of sandpaper glued on. The companies could standardize the "feel labels" and print "feel codes" such as:

Sandpaper	=	Abrasive cleaners
Bumps	=	Oven cleaners
Velvet	=	Air fresheners
Bristles	=	Hair sprays

Isn't that a terrific idea? Of course, it still wouldn't help me—I would have to find my glasses to read the "feel code."

If a blind man leads a blind man, both will fall into a pit. (Matt. 15:14)

I can barely read without my glasses—but, thank the Lord, I am not blind. As my eyesight gets progressively worse, I wonder sometimes, is anything worse than blindness?

Yes. Spiritual eyes that will not see.

The LORD gives sight to the blind. (Ps. 146:8)